Laura López

The Connected and Committed Leader

Lessons from Home. Results at Work.

Laura Lopez

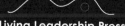

Living Leadership Press

Houston, Texas
2008

Copyright © 2008 Laura Lopez

Living Leadership
P.O. Box 30259
Houston, TX 77249-0259
Fax — 713-864-9356
info@livingleadershippress.com

www.LivingLeadershipPress.com

ISBN# Hardcover — 978-0-9798673-1-6
ISBN# Soft Cover — 978-0-9798673-0-9

Lopez, Laura, 1960 -
   The connected and committed leader / Laura Lopez.
   p. cm.
   Includes bibliographical references.
   ISBN 978-0-9798673-0-9 (pbk.)
   ISBN 978-0-9798673-1-6 (hardcover)

1. Leadership. 2. Management. 3. Organizational effectiveness. I. Title.

HD57.7 L668 2007   658.4/092 22—dc22

Book Packaging Team
Rita Mills — Publishing Consultant & Packaging Coordinator
www.bookconnectiononline.com
Developmental Editing — Denise Barkis Richter, Ph.D.
Content Editing — Debbie Frontiera
Copy Editing — Faye Walker, Ph.D.
Graphic Artist / Cover Design — Teal Marie Chimblo

The paper used in this publication meets the requirements of the American National Standard for Permanence of Paper for Printed Library Materials Z39.48-1984.
Printed in the United States of America

Dedication

To my daughter,

Leila,

who has taught me the true meaning of leadership.

Acknowledgements

This project was a collaborative effort. I had the help of many talented friends and professionals whom I would like to thank.

Denise Barkis Richter, Ph.D., Developmental Editor — Denise is a talented communications professional and a dear friend for over twenty-five years. She is eloquent and artful in her approach to the written word. She masterfully massaged my text so that my messages could have the greatest impact. This book benefited greatly because of her efforts.

Teal Marie Chimblo, Teal Designs, Cover and Logo Design — I met Teal and knew instantly that she had style. She is a multi-faceted and talented woman. In working with her on the book and other aspects of my business, she has brought me one good design after another.

Deborah Frontiera, Content Editor — Debbie reviewed my very first, and raw, manuscript. She was gentle and encouraging in her style of editing. She was exactly what I needed in that moment of time.

Rita Mills, of The Book Connection, Book Design, and Consulting — I met Rita in early 2006 at a National Speakers Association meeting. Rita was there to educate us on the ins and outs of book publishing. My book was already in the works, and I approached her immediately. I knew that she would be great to work with, and I have never looked back. She held my hand every step of the way!

Faye Walker, Ph.D., Copy Editor — When I met Faye, I knew we were supposed to meet. She has lived a block away from me for the past nine years and has an adopted daughter from India. Her editing ensured that I didn't break any of the rules in punctuation and grammar.

To those who took the time to read my many versions along the way to a finished product: Amy Lily, Don Knauss, Larry McWilliams, Joe Scalzo, Abigail Rodgers, Sondra Slappey, Doug Stevenson, Tom Hensler, Christine Graziano Zill, and Lewis Marks.

Lewis Marks, hubby extraordinaire — Support at home is always a welcomed addition to any endeavor. Lewis was great in providing the much-needed neck rubs after long hours on the computer and keeping Leila entertained when I just needed to finish that last paragraph. He is also my in-home computer genius that keeps my technical inabilities in-check!

Table of Contents

The
Connected
and
Committed
Leader

Lessons from Home. Results at Work.

PART I
RATIONALE

Leadership should be born out of the understanding of the needs of those who would be affected by it.

—Marian Anderson

CHAPTER 1

Leadership as a Life Practice for Success

At first glance, applying lessons from home, like parenting, to leadership may seem as odd as pairing home economics with business classes, especially because we often think of leadership as something that takes place outside of the home in a business, political, or military environment. We also think that leadership is for the select few who make it to the proverbial *top*. In contrast, becoming a parent is mostly available to anyone seeking the position and, therefore, it doesn't carry that sense of "exclusivity" that's associated with leadership. Parenting is something that consumes our lives but mainly takes place in and around the home, outside of our work environment. However, since many adults claim a parent as an influential leader in their lives, parenting is in fact a leadership act when done well. Make no mistake; this book isn't about becoming a better parent. It is a book about

> **Leadership is a life practice for success. Leadership and its core principles help us be more effective communicators, build better relationships and ultimately get more of what we want out of life, both in business and in our everyday lives.**

becoming a better leader by borrowing some great gifts and lessons that parenting offers. When defining parenting as a leadership role, we see that leadership is not exclusively for "the top dogs" but for everyone—from the CEO to the individual contributor. Leadership is something that goes beyond the boardroom into everyday life's challenges and opportunities.

Leadership is a life practice for success. Leadership and its core principles help us be more effective communicators, build better relationships and ultimately get more of what we want out of life, both in business and in our everyday lives.

I had focused my 20's, 30's and early 40's on achieving and accomplishing in other realms than the home and family, mainly on my education, my career in business and marketing, and in climbing the corporate ladder. I was able to achieve a high level of success and had the good fortune of leading wonderful teams of people to launch products, build brands and create advertising campaigns. I was able to generate results year after year for two great companies that I worked for during my more than twenty years of corporate experience.

> **When I was promoted to a level where the expectations began to be more about leadership, where you have to rely on your social networks to get results as opposed to bulldogging them through, I found that it was hard to zig when I had learned only how to zag.**

My first six years out of graduate school, I worked with Avon Products in New York City. My last fifteen years were spent with The Coca-Cola Company, where I became a highly successful Marketing Vice President. I have also been fortunate to have had the opportunity to consult with other great companies across a variety of industries after leaving Coke.

Over the course of my corporate business career, I learned how to get results and to get things done, but in retrospect, I wasn't always as effective as I could have been at leading and inspiring others. Somewhere along my climb up the ladder, the "people duties" got relegated to another department called Human Resources. I was so focused on the end results that I wasn't always concerned with the route to get there. I had progressed in my career by accomplishing results and getting things done, and I was rewarded for this. When I was promoted to a level where the expectations began to be more about leadership, where you have to rely on your social networks to get results as opposed to bull-dogging them through, I found that it was hard to zig when I had learned only how to zag. My zagging behavior had been reinforced through financial rewards and promotions.

What I found was that I was managing timelines, projects, deadlines, and people as if they were one and the same. Even when I realized that maybe I might get better results by improving my leadership skills, I was apprehensive. After all, if what I had been doing got me this far, why would I want to change? I was actually afraid of changing. What if I changed the wrong thing? How would I know that a new me would be equally successful? When you are used to getting results one way and being rewarded

> **When a leader overdoes and steps in too much, their people under deliver. I would feel the burn out and I know my teams would lose the zest and passion just watching me burn out after some time.**

for it, it is really tough to change. My "modus operandi" was to persist stubbornly, thinking I could make things happen and get things done. However, this sense of accomplishment caused a great deal of stress and pain along the way. People sweated things out with me, and we weren't always having great fun. I wasn't always enjoying the people or the work, and there were many times that I felt I just couldn't continue the pace. I am also sure that I didn't get the full potential of my team. And sadly, I wasn't in a good position to be able to mentor others.

When a leader overdoes and steps in too much, their people under-deliver. I would feel the burn out, and I know my teams would lose the zest and passion just watching me burn out after some time. This type of high-drive-results-only approach is like running a five-speed car in first gear, revving up and trying to stay with the cars that are on cruise control zooming down the highway. You burn out, and you burn out those around you. I realized that I was good at the sprints—pedal to the metal, all out sprints. However, this approach wasn't sustainable for the long run. Of course, I didn't know it at the time; I was too close to see it. I think many managers today are in that same place. Too close to see it. It is also especially common today to focus on short-term results. Today's business environment has fierce competition and the pressure to attain results is constant. Couple this reality with the fact that there are also fewer and fewer resources to get the job done since downsizing is now a way of life.

The engines certainly are over-revving. The need for leadership is great, but effective leadership is not easy. It is not easy for many reasons, but I think that one of the main reasons that it is difficult is that people really don't understand how to lead—especially while they are doing their *real* job. Anything added on to your already full plate is an overload that isn't very easily taken on. Like great parenting, leadership takes a ton of commitment, compassion and connection. People usually understand why you might be willing to step up to the plate as a parent—after all,

> Once you see and really understand that leadership is the "productivity lubricant" that allows you to get your job done, it is only then that you will be able to do both: your job as you currently define it and your leadership role.

this is your child. But in a work environment, why would you even care so much? You might be wondering then, how in the world can you do your job effectively and also be a great leader? Why should you bother? You have got a job to do, and who has time to baby-sit a bunch of folks? I know that I often had these same concerns when I was asked to attend yet another leadership training class. It was just one more thing to add to my already full plate.

However, once you see and really understand that leadership is the "productivity lubricant" that allows you to get your job done, it is only then that you will be able to do both: your job as you currently define it and your leadership role. If you continue to see leadership as something "outside" of your current work, it will always be an added burden.

> **I saw how parenting was the ultimate leadership experience because it emptomized the tenuous line we all tow as leaders—how to influence and guide behavior without resorting to command and control.**

Changing from how you currently do your job to embracing your full leadership potential will have to be your own personal journey; however, I am happy to share with you my own journey on how I came to understand leadership's importance and to help spur you to realize the same in your own way and at your own pace. As businessman Harold S. Geneen said, "Leadership cannot really be taught. It can only be learned." You have to be ready and open to learn. I am sharing my story as a potential doorway to help you do that.

I spent the bulk of my life where work was my life. My day-to-day existence wasn't focused on being a parent or even thinking about becoming one. For many reasons, including the fact that I wanted to add the parenting role onto my repertoire of experiences, I became a parent at the ripe age of forty-four. This experience at a mature age, after I had already spent more than twenty years in corporate leadership roles, dramatically shifted my view of leadership and inspired me to write this book with the hope of helping others to "get" leadership on a whole different level. After all, like many of you reading this book, I had gone to all of the training. I thought I understood leadership on an intellectual level in my head, but I never did get it at a deeper level. I didn't understand that I needed to lead from the inside out. The lessons of leadership never infiltrated me or caused me to take notice and take it on. I just wanted to get my job done and get on with my work.

Parenting allowed me to really find and open up my heart in a way that it never had before. Being a mediocre parent was not an option. I took the role on as seriously as anyone could ever have, reading up on what the experts recommended and being fully aware of my actions. I had to dig deep within myself to be the best parent I could be. I saw how parenting was the ultimate leadership experience because it epitomized the tenuous line we all tow as leaders—how to influence and guide behavior without resorting to command and control. Everybody and anybody can command and control. It is absolutely easy to demand "I am the boss. Go get this done."

I never thought that I relied on this tactic as much as I did, but I did. Even if I never used those exact words, my actions reflected those thoughts. I could absolutely demand that my three year old follow my commands ("because I said so"), but how could I get a three year old to choose actions that are in line with what I want her to do, while allowing her to be herself and feel good about herself? How do we empower our work associates to seek and find solutions and get things completed in ways that not only meet our expectations but begin to surpass them in ways we could never have imagined?

One simple answer: Leadership.

When I started to see the connections and similarities

between great parenting and great leadership, I found myself analyzing the behaviors that could in essence be replicated from one situation (home) to another (work). However, the more I analyzed, the more I realized that the lines became even more blurred between home and the office. What resulted are my leadership insights that I believe all great parents and great leaders embody. However, these insights are expressed differently in every single person. We each need to do the deep work within ourselves to express these insights in our authentic way. When expressed, these core insights inspire children and co-workers to achieve their full potential.

I found that the core to my insights is the idea of self-centeredness, or lack thereof. Parenting caused me to lose some or a great deal of the self-centeredness that I had been carrying around with me during my more than twenty years of corporate life. After all, corporate culture and our years at school applaud competition and self-centeredness to get ahead. Great parenting and leadership requires giving up our self-centeredness. This is not an easy task. After forty-four years of only having to think about myself, I took on a role that required shifting the focus from me to my child. Fortunately, this shift carried over into my work life.

> After all, corporate culture and our years at school applaud competition and self-centeredness to get ahead. Great parenting and leadership requires giving up our self-centeredness.

People understand the "sacrifice" when they become parents. I can't tell you how many people said to me "Your life will never be your own again." They knew that kids would consume our focus and would force us to shift our priorities. You don't even have to be a parent to understand this. However, I never had anyone say anything similar to me as I climbed the corporate ladder and assumed more and more leadership responsibilities, including people's satisfaction in their work life. This responsibility also requires great sacrifice.

Think about how much time we spend working and how much influence our bosses have on our satisfaction and fulfillment. How much time and energy is spent griping about our bosses?

When you analyze the great leaders of all time, there is no question that they gave all of themselves in their role as leaders. The giving of oneself as a parent is through the act of love, and love should also be in the forefront of great leadership. You also don't need to be a parent to understand it because if you are a human, you will know intuitively how *right* these insights feel. The beauty of great leadership is that it is pure. When you are graced by it, you can't take issue with it. You just want more of it! These insights are hard to argue with because they are simple, basic and logical. They are based in the art of human relating and respect. That doesn't make them easy to employ: it takes a great deal of self-awareness, commit-

> The giving of oneself as a parent is through the act of love, and love should also be in the forefront of great leadership.

> The beauty of great leadership is that it is pure. When you are graced by it, you can't take issue with it. You just want more of it! These insights are hard to argue with because they are simple, basic and logical. They are based in the art of human relating and respect. That doesn't make them easy to employ: it takes a great deal of self-awareness, commitment, and connection to be the leader that you have the power to be.

ment, and connection to be the leader that you have the power to be.

I want to share a personal story that helped me to see the connection between leadership and parenting. It is not that the act of parenting and the act of leading others are one and the same, surely they are not, but rather it is the underlying insights that help people become great parents and those same great insights that help people become great leaders. It was in my quest to become a great parent that I stumbled upon its connection to leadership. The more we are in touch with ourselves, the better parents and leaders we can be. And so the story goes something like this:

My husband and I were in the process of adopting our daughter from Russia. I was forty-four at the time, so clearly I was a mature mom who had dedicated those early baby making years to my career. We had gone through the grueling paper work, interviews, the criminal and psychological testing (yes, we passed!) and even had met our future daughter, Leila, in Yekaterinburg, where she had lived in an orphanage since birth. We were getting ready to bring her back home, and I had planned to take two months off to ensure that we had the time to bond and adjust. My colleagues and my work team were all thrilled for me. The outpouring of their adoption and parenting stories followed. One interaction with a senior leader of my company, who is my age with three kids of his own, impressed me the most. Our interaction went something like this:

Mike: So, Laura you are going to be a Mom?

Laura: Yep, hard to believe—after all this time!

Mike:	Well, I think you will fully enjoy it. Parenting is really so gratifying. But I will tell you, you will find that everything you have learned in the corporate world—you know everything that has contributed to your success here—it just won't work at home.
Laura:	Really? What do you mean by that?
Mike:	Well you know, at work we get things done. We set the plan and make it happen. With kids, it doesn't work that way. Working with kids takes time.
Laura:	Well, Mike, you are really scaring me.
Mike:	Don't worry, you'll be fine. You'll see. You will just be one way here at work, another way at home.

I pondered on that conversation for months while on my journey to Russia and while I was home with my child. Why would certain behaviors that had taken me so far in my career not work at home? Why would I need to be different at home than at work? Why wouldn't new skills of parenting translate at work? I was scared to death that I was going to be the crappiest mom on this planet.

That conversation not only made me more conscious about what would be needed to be a great parent and how some of my behaviors at work wouldn't be effective at home. It also made me wonder why being with bigger people (adults) wouldn't translate when working with children (presumably little people)? Some of it seemed obvious, but some of it just didn't make sense. When had our wires gotten so crossed that our employees were no longer people? When did becoming adults mean that we didn't have the same basic needs as children? Why do we think that the "Look at me Mom. Look at me!" needs expressed by a two year old are that different than someone who is thirty-eight and needs and wants to be recognized for their accomplishments?

We know that kids are people and we treat them like people, but once we are adults, well, we are no longer treated like people, but rather Human Capital. We're tough, right? We can take it. Go ahead and tell me what to do. I will just go ahead and do it. No rebellion, right? Wrong. In fact, this is where kids can actually be easier to manage. Children will tell it to you straight. You absolutely know when a three year old doesn't want to do something that you need to change your approach. Adults say they buy-in and nod their heads in unison, but when it comes time to implement, they are off in some corner bad-mouthing the boss about their stupid idea. Hmmmm. Not easy.

The more I thought about it, Mike was right, management and parenting were diametrically opposed. If you treated kids like a project work plan, you would be in big trouble. Children don't operate well on time clocks. However, Mike was wrong when he said that none of the work skills would serve me at home. If great leadership was present at my workplace and I was a great leader, I would argue that these skills would certainly be applicable to parenting. And vice versa.

> **What I learned at home as a parent could transfer to office leadership situations. After all, both parenting and leadership are disciplines that tap into our hearts.**

What I learned at home as a parent could transfer to office

leadership situations. After all, both parenting and leadership are disciplines that tap into our hearts. They tap into our inner being as a way to connect and commit. So for me, learning to become a more effective parent was one way that I began to learn how to become a more effective leader. What I mean by this is that as a parent, I challenged myself to perfect my human relating skills in ways that I had never challenged myself before, by better reflecting who I was. Parenting requires a tremendous amount of self-awareness and self-discipline. I knew that I had the power to damage someone's life. It also allowed me to see the impact of how my behavior clearly affected another human being. It became evident to me that in order to affect any change outside of ourselves, whether it is for our work success or our personal success, the only change that we can affect is in us, our thoughts, behaviors and actions.

Hence, leadership, like parenting, is all about our thoughts, feelings and actions that influence another to become inspired and motivated, or not. I have quickly learned that you can't make anyone do anything, not even my stubborn three year old, unless you want to strip them of their spirit. We need to remember this. Too many leaders in corporations today believe that they can make people do things. That is already part of the problem. Until we realize that we can only inspire folks to exert their own free wills to do what we want, we will have

> Hence, leadership, like parenting, is all about our thoughts, feelings and actions that influence another to become inspired and motivated, or not.

nay-sayers and a lack of productivity. It is all about how you lead them, and whether you inspire them to do things that are in accordance with their wills and natural gifts.

My insights of leadership as a life practice for success are applicable to any and all relationships in our lives, from spouses or significant others to friendships and professional relationships. Leadership provides the ingredients to influence others in a fruitful, engaging exchange, where people can grow and achieve great things collectively by leveraging their strengths together.

I came from a generation of both men and women who learned that hearts did not have a place in business. Showing any emotion was a sign of weakness; there was no place for it in the board room. So we all put on our corporate armor, and we went to work protected and hidden from ourselves and our hearts. I even went so far as to not socialize with folks at work. It isn't that I was impersonal at work; I just kept a wall up that was palpable and told people "Don't go there." I didn't reveal the real me, and so I could only connect with people to a certain degree. I felt it was important to keep myself removed and not mix my two worlds. I left the most important elements of myself at the corporate door. Like me, we often leave behind the things that make us unique. We shave it off at the door so we can "fit in" and "succeed" through someone else's definition. We are disempowered through this process. I suboptimized my potential as a leader by doing this.

I once asked a boss, "What should I start doing to be more effective?" His response was, "Start being the same person at work as you are at home." I didn't understand it at the time, but what he was telling me was, "Be yourself. Be all of you."

I engaged my head, and only my head, at work. My passions and creativity led a life outside of my corporate world. Sadly, I couldn't see or understand how these other sides of me could be relevant to my work associates or to my work life. After all, business is business. Nothing personal! Right? Wrong.

Business is extremely up front and personal. People do business with people they like. People relate to and want to help other people they enjoy. People build trust with others who don't let them down. Business is very personal. It is not about kissing up and fitting in. It's about being you. Now, if business is very personal, leadership is upfront and intimate. Leadership requires people to connect emotionally. Leadership is about inspiring others. Many corporate environments today need to become more personal. Leaders need to be real people. We don't want scripted robots. We want and need people to connect in the workplace. We need more humanity in our work environments so that people can grow and flourish. Businesses will improve because their people are growing and engaged.

> Now if business is very personal, leadership is upfront and intimate. Leadership requires people to connect emotionally. Leadership is about inspiring others.

When I say that parenting is the ultimate leadership experience, I say it because it really is all about connection and the commitment needed to be focused on the connection. When I took those two months off from work and my husband took another three weeks, we had one critical goal for our daughter, Leila, and that was to have her connect emotionally with us. There was no doubt that we were committed to her. We certainly understood the benefits of this connection. With connection comes trust. With connection comes hope. With connection comes confidence. With connection comes security to take risks. With connection comes growth. And with connection comes freedom to be ourselves.

Leadership requires connection. My hope is to inspire you to embrace the leader in you and to take leadership into every aspect of your life. Lead in parenting. Lead in the boardroom. Lead at everything in between. Let's bring back the humanity that we so desperately need in today's workplace.

Our chief want in life is somebody who shall make us do what we can.

—Ralph Waldo Emerson

CHAPTER 2

Bring Your Heart to Work

When I began getting my thoughts on paper for this book, I asked people to tell me who had inspired them the most in their life. I asked them in planes, at the airport, at the grocery store, in my neighborhood, and wherever I could find someone willing to answer my question. Nine times out of ten, people said "a teacher" or "a parent." Unfortunately, "my boss" didn't make the list. And yet, when we use the word "leader," we suddenly think that it has to be some head honcho running some big corporation. Wrong.

Leadership is about inspiration, and inspiration happens everywhere, not just in the workplace. In fact, my research suggests that it doesn't happen nearly enough in the workplace. I think we get tangled up when we use the word leadership because we have been taught to think that great leaders have to be in big leadership roles. Leadership is more than a role. However, when we look at the outcomes of great leadership, we

> **Leadership is about inspiration, and inspiration happens everywhere, not just in the workplace. In fact, my research suggests that it doesn't happen nearly enough in the workplace.**

intuitively know that leadership is not reserved for the top of a corporation, but that leadership is present in all walks of life.

Through the free teleseminars that I conduct on a weekly basis, my research is continuous. These forums allow me to reach a lot of people. I share my viewpoint and expertise on leadership, and participants raise their questions and concerns on leadership. Go to www.AskLauraLopez.com to post your questions and join me on any of these free, weekly teleseminars. I address five to seven questions during a one-hour session. I would love to hear your questions and comments about leadership.

As I dug deeper and asked people what it was about a person that made them a great leader, they said things like, "She really saw me for who I really am," or "He believed in my potential. It was as if he knew that I had greatness in me," or "She really cared about hearing what I had to say. My perspectives mattered a great deal to her."

Once again, I didn't hear many of these things about a work-related relationship. Most of them were related to deep, personal connections that developed over time in a parent or teacher relationship. Each of these stories existed because someone brought their heart to work. When we see deeply into someone and allow them to shine through, we are suspending all that we are trying to impose on them. This act requires heart.

In my parenting experience, I had a child whom I was discovering. She came with her own little make up, her own little DNA, and her own little past. I suspended what I thought I knew about her and simply tried to see what she wanted to be. When we engage more of our hearts and less of our heads, we allow people to blossom. We can begin to be able to mentor and develop others. In the workplace, we are overly head-driven because we have the deadlines, we have the ways in which we like to see things done, and we don't stop to think that each person working with us needs to be discovered in some way. This requires knowing ourselves from the inside out and bringing our hearts to work. It requires that we see people in the workplace as individuals, not just bodies getting the job done.

Inspirational leaders in the workplace know themselves and are comfortable with being themselves. They care about the people who work for them. My hope is that we can develop more leaders who care about people. My desire is to help transform our work environments so that we can be inspired and inspire others to find their greatness. As I mentioned earlier, I worked for two wonderful companies during my corporate career. Both of these companies often spoke of the importance of leadership. Undoubtedly, they were committed to leadership development. But I can sadly, yet honestly, say that I didn't feel touched by many great leaders during my tenure.

> **This requires knowing ourselves from the inside out and bringing our hearts to work. It requires that we see people in the workplace as individuals, not just bodies getting the job done.**

I didn't see great leadership demonstrated, and I didn't have many role models or mentors in these organizations. This is often the "catch 22" that happens in corporate life. We don't get the love, so we don't give the love. It is a vicious, downward spiral where no one can win. I didn't always feel that my "leaders" were interested in getting to know me or connecting with me personally. I worked for some great people, but few shared any personal stories about themselves and few opened their hearts up to show me who they were.

If there is one thing you take away from this chapter about bringing your heart to work, it is this: the leader always needs to go first. You can't ask of your people to give what you can't give yourself. We often hear today that companies want an engaged workforce. Engagement is as much emotional as it is intellectual. Businesses want employees to love their work, love their jobs, and love their companies. Yet, they don't give the love. So if you want your people to be open and give you their best, be sure to go first and give what you'd like to receive. *You* have to bring your heart to work before you can expect your team to do the same. You have to be a person with humanity and heart. People are inspired by real people. Real people have heart.

When I say "bring your heart to work," I don't mean the easy stuff. Dig deep in yourself and share some core values about who you are and why you are who you are. I remember my mom saying, "Please talk to your brother." She would ask me to talk to my younger and only brother. She would always say, "He listens to you." Apparently, she believed that he wouldn't listen to her. I had a respectful relationship with my brother. I shared more about myself than I told him about himself. I didn't realize that what I was doing was leading my brother. I listened more than I told. I answered only when asked. I respected him, and, in turn, he respected me. Leadership is a two-way street. It breaks down if it is a one-way monologue. The way to start a two-way dialogue is to go first. Go first and be genuine. Bring your heart. When your heart is present, the tone is set. The tone for leadership is based on mutual respect.

> Companies want employees to love their work, love their jobs, and love their companies. Yet, they don't give the love. So if you want your people to be open and give you their best, be sure to go first and give what you'd like to receive. You have to bring your heart to work before you can expect them to do the same.

Just like the saying "Lead by example" advocates, we

do need to be the first ones stepping out of our comfort zone so that others will follow. I use this example in the context of getting to know people personally and to make personal connections. "Share first" is a great rule. You will be amazed at how much people will connect and open up to you once you take the first leap.

I became a better leader the more I let people see all of me. It took a lot of courage to do this. However, the more I invited co-workers into other aspects of my life, the more respect I garnered and the harder they worked for me. They were supporting a person, a person whom they knew and loved. With this perspective, I started to begin to understand why there was such a large gap in leadership despite the fact that many companies focus on leadership development.

> **Just like the saying "Lead by example" advocates, we do need to be the first ones stepping out of our comfort zone so that others will follow.**

Leadership takes heart—a lot of it.

If you are anything like me, you understand leadership intellectually, but you don't embrace it emotionally. I don't think I could have understood it emotionally because I "checked my heart" at the door, and there wasn't much my head could do with the leadership information I was given. I had very few role models, also. After all, we can't motivate and inspire from the head, can we? Those teachers and parents who inspired people didn't do it with their heads; they did it with their hearts. Leadership takes heart—a lot of it.

As my child has grown older, she loves to hear our stories over and over again. She wants me to tell her about the day we met and what we did and how we felt. She loves it. Kids and adults both love to hear personal stories that tell us about each other, demonstrate our values, and show our hearts.

As I ventured down the path of my research, I wondered if I was the only person who had encountered one true leader throughout my entire business career. I asked people how many great leaders they had encountered in their careers.

I got an average of less than one. This meant that many people had zero as their answer, and many had only one as their answer. A minority claimed two or more. Leaders are not plentiful. The reality is that we don't have many great leaders in the work place. As a result, many people don't feel inspired, motivated and appreciated. Their best strengths are not being tapped so they leave big parts of themselves at the door.

> **Kids and adults both love to hear personal stories that tell us about each other, demonstrate our values, and show our hearts.**

Leadership is a choice. Like being a good parent, we must actively commit to being a good leader. It is a courageous choice that we have to make. While most people get a minimum of nine months to prepare for parenting, we sometimes find ourselves thrust into leadership roles at work without any lead time. The best leader we can be is to be our authentic selves. By being ourselves, we give permission for others to do the same. When we are our full selves, we see others more clearly. We become the catalyst for them to be the best they can be.

This is leadership.

Companies want an engaged work force because they want productivity, but leaders at every level don't want to risk showing their hearts. Showing your heart can be frightening. It is safer to put on armor and not be exposed. It is a vicious cycle. Leaders don't bring their authentic selves to work and as a result their team doesn't either.

Nobody wins.

Leaders need to go first. Bring your heart to work and your employees will, too. Other benefits will follow, like dedication, engagement, enthusiasm and innovation. Does this mean that leadership is almost impossible? I don't think it is impossible, but I do believe that it requires some unlearning and some broadening of several concepts. I also think that it takes a lot of courage and a keen understanding of ourselves. It is not easy to bring our hearts to work. I know this from personal experience. When it was time for me to go back to work after two months of bonding with my daughter, I found myself wondering how I could ever be *that* woman that I used to be. I had shed my corporate armor, and I did not want to put it back on. One day, I reflected so much on this that I was a bumbling fool by the time my husband came home. Our conversation went something like this:

> Leadership is a choice. Like being a good parent, we must actively commit to being a good leader. It is a courageous choice that we have to make.

Lewis: You okay hon? What's going on?

Laura: I don't know how to do it anymore. I don't know how I am going to go back to work and be that woman anymore. I don't think I know what to do.

Lewis: Leila is in your heart now and forever. That can't change. You need to bring your heart to work.

Laura: Bring my heart to work? Bring my
heart to work? Are you crazy?

Lewis: Your people need you. They need all of
you. Bring your heart to work.

He was right. I was changed forever. I knew it, and he knew it. I had to have the courage to bring my heart to work. And I bet at that moment that my team would feel the change when I returned to work. I had no choice but to bring my heart to work. When I returned to the office that next week, I realized that I had indeed changed. I found myself listening a bit differently. I found myself more interested in others' perspectives, even if they seemed to be a bit off course, initially. I found that the more I pulled back, the more my team pushed forward. I found myself more willing to allow mistakes to happen despite tight timelines. I second guessed my old habits of setting up meetings at 6 p.m. after a full day had already been clocked. I also found myself opening up more about my new experiences as a mother, which was something that I was desperately afraid of at first. I thought that I might lose my credibility as a business-driving, results-oriented leader if my team saw a softer side of me, but I was so wrong.

> I thought that I might lose my credibility as a business-driving, results-oriented leader if my team saw a softer side of me, but I was so wrong.

What I found instead was that my team and my colleagues expressed a new sense of respect for me that they hadn't expressed before. I was suddenly more human. I was now one of them, particularly the other women on my team who struggled with their working-mom situations. I now was a role model. We connected in ways as a team that I never thought possible. We hit record timelines. We were productive and we had a lot more fun in the process. I was more relaxed, more myself and less guarded. I wondered why it took so long for me to get it. I think people like me actually make it harder for themselves as leaders and as managers when they check parts of themselves at the door. We take ourselves way too seriously and we build too many walls that inhibit others, ourselves and, ultimately, our business. When we set ourselves free, we give permission to others to do the same.

This life-changing event is what tipped the scale for me. What will it be for you? Can you relate to my journey in one small way? I hope so, because if my story takes us to a better place that allows for a healthier work environment with engaged, creative minds that are challenged and appreciated, you just have to believe that magnificent results will be accomplished.

> **I also realized that I had learned so many wrong and outdated concepts about business and leadership and that I had inappropriately applied them for many years during my career.**

In my reflections, I also realized that I had learned so many wrong and outdated concepts about business and leadership and that I had inappropriately applied them for too many years during my career. I learned that you had to direct your people in order to lead. I learned that you had to be tough to be strong. I learned that you had to be in high gear 24/7 to be productive and effective. I learned that as a leader you *made* things happen.

I also know that I wasn't alone in my erroneous beliefs about leadership. Our "leaders" today talk too much and listen far too little. We are so busy "checking off" the to-dos that we do far too little thinking, reflecting and listening. We look for simplification in our work lives by seeking out like-minded thinking instead of challenging ourselves and our businesses with differences.

We have been *lazy* leaders. Then we wonder why we aren't developing the right culture or getting the right long-term results. We wonder why people are burned out, uninspired and jumping ship. Entrepreneurs are the fastest growing business leaders today, particularly women entrepreneurs. Why is this so? Corporate culture is struggling to get results and keep good performers. We wonder why people retire and die two weeks later with massive coronaries. We wonder why people don't feel like they are being seen or appreciated for their strengths.

> I don't support the idea of blaming the top of an organization to impact change. Leadership has to happen at all levels in an organization to effectively impact the whole.

Leadership with heart is the answer to many of these woes. This type of leadership is necessary at all levels. I don't support the idea of blaming the top of an organization to impact change. Leadership has to happen at all levels in an organization to effectively impact the whole. Some myths about leadership must be revealed before we can really start creating better, more effective leaders all around us. Are you ready to be part of the solution? I hope so.

It is better to know some of the questions than all of the answers.

—James Thurber

CHAPTER 3

Busting the Leadership Myth

L eadership is a term that is laden with misunderstanding. Webster's Dictionary defines a leader as "a person followed by others." I would add one word to that definition: "a person followed *voluntarily* by others." As long as we realize that the "following" is voluntary, then we have a leader. This definition goes beyond the "command and control" and the "having to" often imposed by a corporate hierarchy. I said earlier that we can't make people do things, but some people would argue that they are expected to perform some duties in return for their pay/benefits so that they don't really have the choice. In other words, they might not do these things if they were not being told to do them or required to do them for their work. This is in part true, but they do have the choice to keep the job and the choice to show up for the job. They are there by choice.

The thesaurus on my PC says the following terms are synonymous with leadership: Management. Control. Headship. Direction. It is no wonder that there is a great deal of confusion about leadership today. These words are in direct opposition to what leadership is.

At the end of the day, the people who work for us are voluntarily coming there to put in their day. This must never be forgotten. People choose to come to work and people choose to put into work as much as they want to put in. These choices might not all be active, conscious choices, but they are choices we all make with whatever actions we take. By adding the word voluntary in my definition, I am trying to reinforce the fact that actively following another person must be a conscious choice.

> My insights for leadership as a life practice for success are for business and life in the 21st century. We are at a place in time where command and control just doesn't work anymore.

The thesaurus on my PC says the following terms are synonymous with leadership: Management. Control. Headship. Direction. It is no wonder that there is a great deal of confusion about leadership today. These words are in direct opposition to what leadership is. The fact is that we are rewriting the definition of leadership for what is going to be useful in the 21st century. Most of these "synonyms" listed are antiquated. They apply to the command and control model of yesteryear. Leadership has evolved, and it is continuing to evolve. Today, people expect more out of life. People want not only financial satisfaction from their work; they also want emotional satisfaction from their work.

Now Larry Winget might disagree with this. In his book *It's Called Work for a Reason,* he says that we should just "get over ourselves" and accept the fact that we need to work and that work is just that, work. But I think he is remiss not to acknowledge that people expect more today. This is evident in many of the trends that the boomer generation is setting. Retirement is being redefined as a second career. Retirement property goes beyond Florida and into areas of the world like Costa

Rica, Panama and Honduras. There are fewer boundaries and borders to how we define life.

My insights for leadership as a life practice for success are for business and life in the 21st century. We are at a place in time where command and control just doesn't work anymore. We have more choices and we want to exercise those choices. Gone are the days of just doing "what we are supposed to do." Thankfully, we are starting to take the "shoulds" out of our vocabulary and out of our lives. People are starting to redefine their own lives and are taking on a greater level of responsibility to live their own lives with full intention and conscious choice. Slowly, we are seeing that command and control ways of leadership are ineffective and don't allow creativity or diversity to contribute to more robust work environments.

I believe that the companies that get this will be the ones leading the way into the future. I love to use Southwest Airlines as an example. Southwest's whole business model and culture is based on freedom. Freedom to allow people of all economic backgrounds access to travel through cheaper fares. Freedom to be who you are as an employee, and freedom from the hierarchies in decision-making that stifle many companies today. Southwest embodies freedom in every aspect of their business. They give their passengers the freedom to sit where they want to, and the freedom to change their flights without penalty.

Over time, other company cultures started to strip away some of the superficial formality of our businesses with business casual dress and dress-down Fridays. It was all an attempt to bring some approachability into our business relationships.

I fly a great deal for my business, and I have traveled extensively for more than thirty years. I believe there is a palpable difference in the "air" of Southwest Airlines when compared to other air carriers. The people who work at Southwest are happy when you fly their airline. You can feel the cultural difference when you travel Southwest versus other carriers. The people who serve you at Southwest are relaxed, comfortable and seem to be enjoying themselves at work.

At first, in the early '90s, I thought it was a bit hokey, since attendants were so overly casual for the time. But they were trend setters. Formality is an antiquated carry-over from the command and control ways. It can inhibit the personal connections we seek with great leadership. Over time, other company cultures started to strip away some of the superficial formality of our businesses with business-casual dress and dress-down Fridays. It was all an attempt to bring some approachability into our business relationships. We wanted to be seen as real people.

Stripping out formality was also evident in our effort to alter our physical work environments into cubicles. We broke down physical walls so that we could start working more effectively across groups. I was never in full support of the cubicle approach to business office layout. People need some privacy and some quiet to get their work done. This forced approach to get people to talk and to work out problems in person overlooked the realities of the day-to-day business needs. However, I do fully endorse equal size offices across the board. I think any effort to get leaders to learn from their people without placing additional barriers between them should be applauded.

A personal story comes to mind here, borrowing again from my parenting experience. When it was time for me to go back to work, I had to find the perfect nanny to entrust the care and development of my daughter. I took the hiring route that I grew accustomed to in my corporate roles. I employed a search agency to screen and represent candidates interested and qualified for the position. The agency matched my requirements against their talent and forwarded me the resumes that met my criteria. After reviewing resumes and culling them down, I then spent some screening time on the phone before narrowing the interview pool down to five people. I planned the interview during my daughter's nap time so that I had quality time with each candidate. But I also planned the interview late enough during Leila's nap time so the candidate could meet my daughter, and I could observe some of her behaviors with my child. I was looking for some very specific things in my candidates. I was looking to see how this adult would approach my child. Was she going to impose herself on the child or would she let the child come to her? What this meant to me was that she was going to allow my child to assert herself and that she would not impose her reality onto my child. I also purposely placed Leila on the ground and sat down with her to see how the nanny would react. I would clearly invite the nanny to come forward, thus giving her a green light to interact. Would she get down on her hands and knees to interact with Leila, or would she continue sitting on the couch and remain removed from the interaction? I learned a great deal from this "test" with the folks I interviewed.

I knew that the kind of "leader" I was looking for would be someone who would allow my child to come into her own on her own terms, and she would also be the kind of leader who would get down into the dirt to relate to her.

> It is only from a position of strength and confidence that you are truly able to allow others to be themselves. Your position of authority is not threatened by the fact that you aren't in need of proving that you are the boss. You can, in fact, "be one of them."

There is a common misperception that surfaces when I describe these qualities in a leader and/or in a parent. Some believe that I am suggesting that you just be friends with your child or your associates. This is not the case. Befriending implies that you will alter your behavior so that you are liked. This means that you have the wrong focus, which is you. *You* want to be accepted and liked.

In contrast, my approach places the focus on them, not you. In fact it is only from a position of strength and confidence that you are truly able to allow others to be themselves. Your position of authority is not threatened by the fact that you aren't in need of proving that you are the boss. You can, in fact, "be one of them".

Leadership and its principles are directly linked to personal success. Leadership, after all, is relevant to all of us, because we live in a world full of people. Whether you want to do business with someone, or influence them, or sell to them, important leadership skills based on the human psychology of relating are key. I want to cut through the things that leadership is not. By dispelling every myth of what leadership is, a new definition emerges. This myth busting is the foundation for building leadership insights as a life practice for success.

Leadership is not about *doing*, it is about *being*.
Leadership is not about *directing*, it is about *guiding*.
Leadership is not about *getting*, it is about *giving*.
Leadership is not about *telling*, it is about *listening*.
Leadership is not about *judging*, it is about *accepting*.
Leadership is not about *driving*, it is about *yielding*.
Leadership is not from the *head*, it is from the *heart*.

There is no doubt that there are times in business when it is all about doing, directing, getting, telling, judging, driving, and engaging our heads. These are all critical skills that are needed to be successful in business and in life in general. However, most of these are not effective when motivating and inspiring people. Much like we need men and women to make the world go 'round, we also need the head and the heart applied in business. Being too skewed to one extreme is detrimental to the whole. The 21st century will require a more holistic, integrated approach that relies on both ends of the spectrum. Businesses have been overly skewed to the directing and doing side to the exclusion of the guiding and being side, and we need to come a bit more to the center with some balance and better integration of the whole.

> Much like we need men and women to make the world go 'round, we also need the head and the heart applied in business. Being too skewed to one extreme is detrimental to the whole.

There is a reason for the clamoring that we are hearing in the business world today about the need for more effective leadership and an engaged workforce. This is a battle cry for some connectivity to ensure that people can work effectively and productively together. Businesses need the results that engaged people bring to the table. We have over-learned that business is all about logic, rational thinking and doing. Unfortunately, we have taken this to the extreme. As I mentioned in the introduction, we need to view leadership as an enabler to our jobs, as our "productivity lubricant." It is not something separate from our doing, directing and driving. I like to think of it as the oil in the engine of a car composed of nuts, bolts, pistons, and spark plugs. The oil, as we know, is essential, but it is simply the lubricant that makes the other parts function effectively. Unfortunately, in businesses today, we often see that the people or "softer" stuff relegated to somewhere else, often to Human Resources. "Oh, you folks take it; it's way too tricky for us people running the business." I know. I used to be one of those line people with Profit and Loss accountability that didn't have time for the people stuff; it got in the way of the real business!

How scary but true. When we finally realize that everything happens through people and that we are all in the people business, we won't separate the two as much as we do today. I am hoping that we can skip lawsuits as catalysts for setting up proper focus on leadership and people.

We live in an increasingly insecure world. People want to have connections. Consumers want to be connected emotionally to the products they buy, and they want these products to stand for humanistic and responsible values. People want to work for companies that give them a place where they feel they can belong. It is our job as leaders to adapt and adjust in order to inspire the best from our people. If you constantly expect people to adjust and adapt to you and your company, then you will never get them to engage to the fullest of their abilities.

> **We live in an increasingly insecure world. People want to have connections. Consumers want to be connected emotionally to the products they buy, and they want these products to stand for humanistic and responsible values. People want to work for companies that give them a place in which they feel they can belong.**

Management is doing things right. Leadership is doing the right things.

—Peter Drucker

CHAPTER 4

Leadership vs. Management:
Two Sides of a Coin

There is an interesting dilemma inherent in our corporate culture today. As people accomplish more individually, they are promoted more often. As they are promoted higher and higher, they eventually become tomorrow's leaders. Yet the transitions from individual contributor to business manager to leader can be very difficult. When we are conditioned to drive the business and get results at all costs, we don't always learn how to get results through others. We have people in leadership roles acting like individual contributors, and we have people in leadership roles who go to the other extreme and rely completely on their employees to bring in the results.

> The truth is that there is a delicate balance between this continuum of doing and inspiring.

The truth is that there is a delicate balance between this continuum of doing and inspiring. Leaders ultimately have to "do" to achieve results, but they do it through others. Therefore, their results are based upon the performance of others, but they do not wash their hands from the responsibility of getting the results.

When Mike told me "Nothing that you have learned at work will work at home with kids," I suspect that what he was referring to were the skills of a project manager, such as setting timelines, directing activities and monitoring progress. I agree that Mike was absolutely right about that. If I were to try to work with my child like a project timeline, I am certain that I would fail. However, if Mike had been referring to the leadership skills of guiding, listening, accepting and yielding, then I believe that a great many of those skills would have been, and, in fact, are, applicable to proper parenting.

When we are in the mindset of a project manager, which many of us find ourselves in when we are driving for results and accomplishments, leadership skills feel counterintuitive and "soft." The trick is to harmoniously blend the two sides of the coin in a way that isn't overly hard-nosed nor too soft and cushy. This is where leadership becomes more of an art than a science. We need people to maintain their results-driven approaches but incorporate some of the elements of effective human relating skills that will allow us to get the most out of people. The beauty of this is that it becomes a win-win. This is how we can get more employees engaged, happy to produce, and satisfied with their work.

> We need people to maintain their results-driven approaches but incorporate some of the elements of effective human relating skills that will allow us to get the most out of people.

The skills of an effective leader, like an effective parent, will draw on the emotional connection and trust that has been built over time to motivate and inspire team members toward a common goal. It is only through others that a leader can meet goals. "Winning ways" for a project manager or an individual contributor are tough behaviors to suddenly stop. The mindset and focus shift need to occur so that a true leader will emerge. The focus on "me" in order to get results needs to shift to "you." Leaders need to unlearn some things as they go forward. Otherwise we begin to see "Leaders" who micromanage. We see "Leaders" who impose their ways to the detriment of the team's creativity. We experience "Leaders" who take all the juice out of their people because they can only see it one way, their way. I don't think it is completely their fault. We have been rewarding them and promoting them for this behavior.

It is really tough to change.

Some businesses are better at grooming leaders than others. Some are not promoting the hard-driving, results-at-all-cost people. I applaud that. Organizations need to look at why they promote people and the messages they send with these promotions. In my work with companies, I have found that companies often say one thing and then do another. This is not too unlike consumers, who say one thing and then do something else with their dollars. You can only believe actions. Words are cheap. Organizations that don't reward leadership behaviors don't have leaders running their organizations. They have high-paid project managers who create poisonous, unhealthy work environments. Employees don't thrive in these environments and neither do business results.

> Organizations that don't reward leadership behaviors don't have leaders running their organizations. They have high-paid project managers who create poisonous, unhealthy work environments.

I can personally identify with many of these issues. I was a hard-driving, results-oriented project manager. I loved to see the impact of my actions by getting projects going and seeing new products I developed on the market. I thrived on that. I was given an opportunity of a lifetime back in 2000 to help start a business venture. This was something that had been attempted before, but it had never fully succeeded. I was working for the Minute Maid division of The Coca-Cola Company, and I was relatively new to the orange juice side of the business. I had spent six years on the carbonated soft drink side of the business. Four of those six years, I was on The Coca-Cola Classic brand team, the flagship brand. During those six years, I got a full picture and understanding of how the overall Coca-Cola system worked, the company and its bottlers. I was asked to bring my expertise and knowledge of that system to bear on this new venture that Minute Maid was embarking upon.

The vision of this new venture was to take the Minute Maid brand into the enormous Coca-Cola Bottling system trucks and distribution system. It would take Minute Maid from refrigerated carton, in-home use to being more readily available in many more points of distribution for on-the-go consumption. This venture was perfect for me. A challenge that promised "this has never been done" was enough for me to sign on. I knew I could get it done! My bull-dogged persistence worked wonderfully with the bottlers, but I quickly learned that I made enemies both at the Coca-Cola headquarters and the Minute Maid offices. I was only focused on getting the job done, and I sure did get it done. The business grew from next-to-nothing to well over $100 million in bottom line profit in a very short time period. But I don't think that I built the necessary connections that I needed for long-term sustainability. After three years of growth, we then saw precipitous declines as other internally competing products started to take precedence. Nobody cared that these competing initiatives were taking focus away from my product lines. My then-boss pulled me aside one day and proceeded to tell me that I was perceived as a non-team player.

Me, a non-team player!

You can imagine my outrage. I had worked so hard to make this new venture happen. I felt that the results we had achieved had, in essence, "saved" several years. As a result, the division benefited and we all got tremendous bonuses for two or three years in a row. I had no clue how in the world I was not perceived as a team player. As it turned out, they were right. I was so focused on my business that my focus was piercing. My colleagues didn't think that I cared two cents about the impact I had on their business, and they felt that I had drawn a line around my team and my business and this was all that mattered.

Were they right? You bet. If I had been the CEO of a small business, that would have been fantastic behavior, but the reality was that I was living within a much larger organization and my eyes were only on my small piece of the pie, my turf. This is a classic problem we see with leaders who haven't fully made the transition from project manager to leader. I was the best project manager, who was also a good leader working effectively with my immediate team, but I wasn't a broader leader in the larger scheme of my organization. I learned this the hard way. In my heart, I wish that my managers had helped me grow and see the importance of the other

> **Folks who are trying to do everything on their own and are so focused on the end result are likely to pass on this highly important yet non-urgent activity.**

businesses. When I went to a more senior colleague who I know wanted to help me, he told me to take a look at Stephen Covey's third habit in *The 7 Habits of Highly Effective People.* Like many results-driven people, I learned that I didn't prioritize relationship building. Covey puts this skill in the non-urgent but highly important category. Folks who are trying to do everything on their own and are so focused on the end result are likely to pass on this highly important yet non-urgent activity. This was a great lesson for me.

So how do we take good project managers who are getting great business results through hard-driving business management approaches and teach them to overlay more effective human relating skills? How do we help them find connection with others so that they can align, inspire and motivate them toward a common goal? First, we need to measure and reward this behavior consistently. We can't promote people until they have demonstrated these skills. We can't perpetuate the cycle of poor leadership. Having folks in leadership roles who don't exhibit effective leadership behaviors hurts the entire organization.

Until we fundamentally believe that we absolutely need great leadership to achieve sustainable results, the short-term fixes will always prevail. We need to put our money and actions where our mouths are. Fundamentally, businesses today need a more holistic and humanistic approach. It is getting harder to get results. People expect more from their companies and their management. Hard-nosed, results-only approaches are outdated, and the model doesn't work anymore! Businesses are looking for sustainable, great results over the long haul, but you can't achieve this without great leadership. The health of a corpo-

> Hard-nosed, results-only approaches are outdated, and the model doesn't work anymore! Businesses are looking for sustainable, great results over the long haul, but you can't achieve this without great leadership.

rate culture should be a metric that is measured and valued. Leadership needs to be present along many levels of an organization. Accountability for leadership also must be present along the many levels.

Marcus Buckingham makes the distinction between managers and leaders by saying "When you deal with people, you manage. When you want to lead, you start with the big picture." I don't fully agree with his distinction. While leadership does require having a big picture, it is not devoid of dealing with people. The powerful leader is focused on the person, the individual. Even when he can't physically touch each and every individual, his actions cascade to many. The leader also must focus on the larger picture of what success looks like for the organization. But the big picture is about strategy, not leadership. Leadership has to help connect the strategy to the individual. You can only do this by focusing on the individual and knowing what is important to the individual. I believe that General Schwarzkopf's quote "You manage things. You lead people" is a much more accurate depiction of the difference between management and leadership. Managers are focused on the achievement/accomplishment side of the equation. Leaders are focused on the experience/engagement side of the equation. Leaders draw on emotion and inspiration. Managers draw on project timelines and execution. We need to do both, but we need to know when to shift gears and strike a balance. A manager doesn't need to know how to lead. A leader has to know how to manage and how to lead.

Execution is still a responsibility of leadership. As Ram Charan points out in his book *Execution,* "Getting things done

> **A manager doesn't need to know how to lead. A leader has to know how to manage and how to lead.**

through others is a fundamental leadership skill. Indeed, if you can't do it, you're not leading. Yet how many leaders do you see who cannot?" Leaders get things done, they don't **do it.** But in order for them to get things done, they need to work through their social networks and bring out the best in people and motivate them toward achieving results. Charan clearly is reminding us not to forget the two pieces. A great leader needs to have the skills to inspire, motivate and bring out the best in people, but she or he must also be grounded in execution, which is the reason for leadership. A great leader achieves results through others and through leadership skills. Leaders can't leave the execution details to others to worry about. Leaders need to know how to use their leadership skills to motivate groups of people to get the needed results. Unlike the manager who achieves results alone without having to rely on the important social network of others, the leader knows the two sides of the coin are inextricably linked.

> A great leader needs to have the skills to inspire, motivate and bring out the best in people, but she or he must also be grounded in execution, which is the reason for leadership.

For a moment, I would like to transition to the female leader. I think women in business have an even harder time than men in understanding these two sides of the coin and how to combine them effectively. I say this from my personal experience as a woman in business. Despite how far we have come, women in business still have to work hard at adapting to masculine-driven corporate cultures that are required to succeed in business. Much of the adapting that the female leader does is voluntary and is based on her own perceptions of her environment. She can overcompensate so much on the business side that any connection to her humanistic or personal side is often perceived as a threat to her success. She believes she has to be tougher, more driven and more decisive than a man to succeed. She can be more "male" than her male counterparts. She believes that because business is business, there is no place for her more vulnerable, feminine side. She actually abandons any and all relating traits that might bring out her vulnerability in this male-dominated business domain.

By doing this, she is actually minimizing her effectiveness. The result is usually disastrous. Not only does she not fully realize her potential as a great leader, but everyone suffers as a result. Those who work for her and around her suffer because she is often the toughest of the lot. She is not a woman who can mentor other women because she is so hardened that she loses compassion for others; ironically, she is also unappealing to the men she works with and for. From every angle, she is isolated. She doesn't bring her full self to work because she sees this as a threat. She feels unsafe in doing so, and yet her full self could bring great benefit to her company and to her work teams.

> She can overcompensate so much on the business side that any connection to her humanistic or personal side is often perceived as a threat to her success. She believes she has to be tougher, more driven and more decisive than a man to succeed. She can be more "male" than her male counterparts.

We can't blame her entirely; organizations need to take responsibility for the women who are like this. They are the product of their environment. Unfortunately, these women are the result of an unbalanced culture. They are a true reflection of a company that does not have any balance between the two sides. You will often find more of these women leaders in companies that also have issues of inclusion and diversity. An unbalanced company culture has many negative side effects. It should be the goal of any company that finds itself in an unbalanced state to strive for a balance that will yield many benefits in its people, its creativity, its engagement and, ultimately, its results.

While I describe these phenomena from a woman's point of view, by no means is it exclusive to women. Other minorities and men can also fall "victim" to this mentality. This is one of the reasons that I personally had difficulty sharing my experiences with adoption and parenting in the work place. I had worked hard to create an all-business image for myself. I wanted people to believe that I could be as tough as any man and that I placed work at the highest of levels of importance. It was hard to let that image go, but in the end, when I was able to reveal the more vulnerable, softer side of who I am, my teams and those around me came to respect me far more than ever before.

> An unbalanced company culture has many negative side effects. It should be the goal of any company that finds itself in an unbalanced state to strive for a balance that will yield many benefits in its people, its creativity, its engagement and, ultimately, its results.

Companies that are bound up in this problem can transition out of it, but it takes focus, commitment and time. Leadership must realize that the culture will initially reject this change because allowing the "softer side" will be viewed as a great risk to its people managers. In essence, we are asking people to let down their guards, to be vulnerable. The current culture was defined and supported by behaviors that didn't require vulnerability, openness or connectivity. Great leadership requires both vulnerability and openness. Vulnerability brings out the best in people. Leaders need to be real people sharing real stories. This takes courage and it also takes a supportive environment that understands the long-term benefits of growing great leaders. We know that this takes time, risk, long-term effort and a great deal of culture change. People often chuckle at this idea and say that we now need to sit around singing "Kumbaya," but as I mentioned earlier, it is situational. There is a time for everything: a time for toughness and a time for bonding. Incorporating both leadership and management principles effectively is what will make companies stronger.

> In essence, we are asking people to let down their guards, to be vulnerable. The current culture was defined and supported by behaviors that didn't require vulnerability, openness or connectivity. Great leadership requires both vulnerability and openness.

Everyone should be respected as an individual,
but no one idolized.

—Albert Einstein

CHAPTER 5

Why Real Leaders Don't Have
Inclusion Issues

Companies have lost millions in lawsuits. People have low engagement with the companies they work for which also costs companies millions in lack of productivity, retention issues and mediocre results. Inclusion is a real issue facing many companies today. Inclusion has been called "diversity" in the past and has traditionally been defined by race, gender and age. I don't like using the term "diversity" for this reason. Inclusion is the result that we are looking for, and it goes beyond attaining the numbers to get there. Inclusion is much, much more. Inclusion is about leveraging differences and finding creative synergy through those differences. Last time I checked, white men were different, too, yet they would generally not be included in "diversity" discussions. How absurd that they weren't included! I know many white males who have also suffered from exclusion as have many women and minorities.

Leveraging differences that matter is how businesses become stronger. We need to bring in our differences from a point of view that is based on our uniqueness and personal experiences. We all know that people are different. Even if you come from similar backgrounds, people are different. Everyone is different. We all interpret the world around us with our unique twist. Thank goodness! What a boring place this would be if we were all the same.

If you don't believe me, just ask your Mom. She knows how different you are from your siblings, or how different you are from your Dad. She will know the little subtleties of difference. Not just the simple things like the foods you like to eat, but the ways in which you think and the ways in which you are unique. Observing, recognizing and leveraging differences shows great leadership in parenting. Inclusion and leadership are linked because you wouldn't have inclusion issues if you were a great leader and you had developed great leaders below you. Why? Because great leaders connect with individuals. Great leaders see each person for who they are and what they can bring to the table. Great leaders are like great parents or great teachers: they bring out the best in people, one person at a time. They recognize and leverage differences. How could you have inclusion issues if you had great leaders throughout the organization? You can't.

> Great leaders are like great parents or great teachers: they bring out the best in people, one person at a time. They recognize and leverage differences. How could you have inclusion issues if you had great leaders throughout the organization? You can't.

Early in my career, I went to Human Resources to complain about a male colleague who, in my opinion, was "poisoning" the environment of a broader team. My complaint about this colleague was that he was not inclusive. His behavior openly ridiculed people in a frat-like way, which visibly disturbed people and didn't foster a team environment. He also had his favorites, and this had some pretty evident ramifications. Those not on his favorite list felt like they "didn't stand a chance," and they didn't bring their best to the table. They felt as though they never would be good enough. He brought with him his personal biases and preferences. What he didn't realize was that he was breeding an environment of fear and non-inclusiveness that stifled learning, risk-taking and long-term results.

This "anti-leadership" behavior worked against the very basic principles of leadership: to motivate and inspire people to bring their best to the table so that they were more engaged and committed to their work. My colleague was great at management and getting short-term results, but he failed miserably at the people-relating skills needed for effective leadership. In fact, some people could have taken some of his actions and said that they were "discriminating."

He was deeply insecure, and he prevented others around him from succeeding. He hid behind his success, and the only people who survived around him were those who were loyal to him. If people disagreed or were different in their approach and style, he found a way to get back at them. Having experienced this person's tactics, I realized that if you succeed at having great leaders who see the potential in all people, there couldn't be such a thing called discrimination. When companies breed good leaders, it becomes a positive upward spiral, a "win-win" all around.

> **People feel good because they feel appreciated for the unique strengths they bring; the company benefits because their employees have their hearts and souls in the work. Results are good, which reinforces and rewards people.**

People feel good because they feel appreciated for the unique strengths they bring; the company benefits because their employees have their hearts and souls in the work. Results are good, which reinforces and rewards people.

Sounds simple, but unfortunately, what happened in this real-life situation wasn't so positive. When I went to this Human Resources manager to express my concern, they told me off the record "It's best to back down on this one. Senior management is willing to look the other way because he is generating such strong business results." What that said to me was that my then-company was giving lip service to inclusion and leadership. They weren't willing to insist that this associate got better at leading. They were willing to focus on the short-term results. While leadership training was put on his development plan, did they really help him get better? His behavior was promoting a culture of fear, exclusion and risk aversion. Not exactly sustainable. My colleague, like many others who were very effective managers, needed to see that the very skills that were making them productive and effective managers weren't going to make them great leaders. You can't grow great leaders overnight; it takes a long-term commitment, as does the understanding that skills in one area aren't necessarily transferable to another.

> You can't grow great leaders overnight; it takes a long-term commitment, as does the understanding that skills in one area aren't necessarily transferable to another.

The one great leader I knew in my career was Don Knauss. Don's leadership skill was evident because not only did Don know your name, he also knew something personal about you and he knew what your strengths were. Don understood the value of great leadership, and he tried hard to be the best leader he possibly could be. When you met Don, you wanted to give him your best because he knew you would. Don would always say, "People want to do their best work."

He believed this, but more importantly, he believed it for you. Don always gave you his best. When he was with you, you felt like the only person in the room. He engaged with you so deeply that you wanted to climb that mountain for him. You wanted to be on his team. You knew that Don knew you wanted to give your best.

Great leaders have faith in people. They don't come from a perspective of "prove it" first. They come from a perspective that honors where you have come from and that believes you will put your best forward. Don had a high bar, but he always came to the party knowing you could reach the bar. Only you had to prove that you couldn't; he believed that you could.

> Great leaders have faith in people. They don't come from a perspective of "prove it" first. They come from a perspective that honors where you have come from and that you will put your best forward.

Great leaders see the upside in people, not the downside. Great leaders are optimistic about people. Like a great parent, they see the potential, not the gap. They see what you could be in a way that still honors who you are today. They see A's on your report card and don't harp on the B's and C's. They know how to focus on your strengths, not bury your nose in the "opportunities." Don knew that you would bring your best each day and every day, and he inspired you to do so.

In my more than twenty years of corporate work, Don has been the only leader who I felt knew me. Therefore, I wanted to work for him. Leadership has an optimistic stance, a rose-colored view, not unrealistic, but optimistic.

Where do companies fail when they have leaders like Don Knauss? They fail at embodying leadership at all levels of the organizations. People quit managers, not companies and certainly not leaders. People generally sue companies for the actions of their managers. Inclusion issues happen one person at a time, one interaction at a time. Companies can't win at building a diverse, creative culture without first succeeding at placing leaders at all levels. Even the individual contributor in an organization needs to embody leadership qualities. While it all starts with the top, having one great leader is not enough. Companies need to build ranks and files of great leaders all the way through to the "street level." Until this happens, real inclusion and creativity can't flow in an organization.

To make this happen, it takes a long-term commitment to building great leaders, one at a time. When Don headed the Minute Maid business unit for The Coca-Cola Company, he insisted that we have certain character traits included in our screening process for new employees. The one that he had a great deal of passion for was what he called "Fire in the belly." This was a trait and not a skill. It was an attitude that he felt contributed to successful business leaders. "Fire in the belly" meant you had it in you to do what was right, that you had the passion in you to be committed and connected to the people and the business. Having the right people on board is critical.

> The model of "up or out" is flawed and no longer relevant in today's business environment. The unfortunate consequences of an "up or out" mentality is that companies end up with a bunch of ego-centric achievers without leadership skills.

To instill a culture change, you have to look critically at who you have in place. As Jim Collins says in *Good to Great*, you have to have the right people on the bus. Some people can't, and, quite frankly, don't want to be in leadership roles. There are folks who are incredible individual contributors who don't want to make the changes to a leadership role. They shouldn't be penalized for this. Let them play to their strengths. I believe that you can reward performance without making everyone take on a leadership role.

The model of "up or out" is flawed and no longer relevant in today's business environment. The unfortunate consequences of an "up or out" mentality is that companies end up with a bunch of ego-centric achievers without leadership skills. "Up or out" cultures aren't building leaders; they are just weeding out the ones who have the guts to say they don't want to be leaders. Companies have to have the discipline and the stomach to pass on the "flash and sizzle" of great short-term producers and know how to sort through their people who really exhibit leadership potential. Generally speaking, these people are well-liked, and they are not always the flashy charismatic type. As Jim Collins identifies in his book *Good to Great*, effective leaders are humble, less ego-driven than many folks who end up in senior positions. Many of the characteristics that Jim Collins uncovered in what he called "Level 5 leaders" are qualities of connected and committed leaders who employ the heart-driven skills necessary to be effective in motivating and inspiring others. Organizations need to really weed out the poison. A great manager who isn't prepared for leadership but who takes on a leadership role can be poisonous to an organization. The poisonous ones can infect a whole division.

On the other hand, as a middle management leader, you can impact your piece of the puzzle. You don't have to wait to have a great leader above you to start your own leading. I think it is a missed opportunity when people don't hold true to their own ways of connecting, and when they aren't getting the love from above, they hold out on their own teams. I know that I didn't always feel that my leaders were leading me, but I didn't want to sell out my team, and so they got the best that I could be most of the time. I am not fault proof. I made mistakes, too. I forgot that leadership went in all directions, not just downward to our teams. But I impacted what I could, and I know that it made a difference to me and to those I led. In the end, that is all that really matters to me.

Great leaders need to have a close ear to the ground to know what their people inherently know. The result of having poor people leaders is like having poor teachers. You get the "A" student who now surprisingly starts to go below average or fails. How in the world does this happen? Often parents wrongly assume that their kids are screwing up. I submit to you that schools fail great students just like companies fail great people. I have seen many great contributors failed by the best of companies. I would look closely at the teachers and the school to understand their biases and their non-inclusive ways. Sometimes if you look a bit closer, it isn't about the child but the environmet.

> I think it is a missed opportunity when people don't hold true to their own ways of connecting, and when they aren't getting the love from above, they hold out on their own teams.

Likewise, companies need to be mindful of their cultures, which can be poisonous, and they need to realize that not only are they not getting the best out of their people, they are shutting down others and misjudging many. This all can happen with one failed manager who needed to be a better leader or perhaps not even placed in a leadership role. One person at a time; every interaction counts. All of this becomes an inclusion issue. I have a lot of faith in a lot of people. I think people, when they are allowed to bring forward the best strength they have, will blow most people away. We just don't ever let them.

How can great leadership overcome this? Great leadership means that we connect at an individual level. This takes precious time that many choose not to dedicate to the area of people. It requires people managers to move from project managers to leaders by not only knowing their people professionally but personally. It requires organizations to be diligent and focused so that they won't tolerate anything but great leadership.

Bureaucracy is often at odds when dealing with the individual. As organizations become more bureaucratic in their approach, the harder it is to build leadership. Bureaucracy works against the principles of leadership in that it tries to boil people down to the lowest common denominator instead of building on individual strengths. Bureaucratic systems that don't serve the organization need to be stripped away to help foster a culture where leadership can flourish. We need to be mindful with every interaction. Respect needs to flow both ways in order for leadership to flourish. We need to honor human beings.

> **Bureaucracy is often at odds when dealing with the individual. As organizations become more bureaucratic in their approach, the harder it is to build leadership.**

Hierarchy can sometimes work against this. The top starts to lose touch with reality, thinking that they really are better than others "below" them. This is very dangerous. An attitude of superiority has no place in a culture where leadership flourishes. In Anthony Smith's book *The Taboos of Leadership,* he speaks about many of the trappings of power. Superiority and entitlement can often come with the territory. I believe there is another way.

> **An attitude of superiority has no place in a culture where leadership flourishes.**

Whether you changed the light bulbs in Don's office, or you were setting the long term strategy for the company, Don knew your name and something about you. Many companies and their top executives have lost their humanity and respect for the person behind the role. It means that we need to understand the context from which our people come. But first we need to share a bit of ourselves with our people before we can ever expect them to do the same. Let them know where you grew up, where you went to school, how you view the nature of work, how you view authority and power, and other, simple things like how many siblings you have, how many children you have, how you view the challenge of parenting or living alone, and what you like to do in your spare time. Don shared a lot about his family, and Ellie, his wife, was one of us. The company loved her equally. They were a team, and we saw it. Don showed us that he was a loving husband and father. We respected that. He brought his full self to work. We honored that.

We need to bring curiosity back when we deal with people. People are afraid to get to know each other and open up personally. Ironically, being so afraid of asking "the wrong questions" for fear of discrimination has isolated all of us in corporations. I spent nearly fifteen years in my last company which is still skewed toward the achieving, management side of the equation. For most of my time there, I was a single woman. I had many managers during that time. Only one manager over that time ever ventured to really open up and tell me about himself. In time, he asked me about my personal life. Did I have someone special

> **We need to bring curiosity back when we deal with people. People are afraid to get to know each other and open up personally. Ironically, being so afraid of asking "the wrong questions" for fear of discrimination has isolated all of us in corporations.**

in my life? Did I some day want to get married? To this day, I consider this manager a friend. He connected with me in ways that other managers never had. I opened up and shared personal stories with him about how I did really want to have children. I can say that he really knew more about my personal motivators and their context than any other manager had before or since. I am certain that others may have wanted to know more about me, but they were reluctant. Clearly, we had to develop rapport first. He had to be vulnerable and open up before I ever would.

The humanistic side of our business has suffered because of the fear of retaliation and litigation. The walls we have built to protect us also create an environment where it is difficult for people to bring out their best. There are ways to ask more personal questions of others that can gauge us on how to respect them and learn from them. People feel and know intent intuitively. If you are asking from a place of genuine curiosity and a willingness to adjust and be receptive to that person, it will not be a dangerous place. But if the questions are coming from a biased place or from an interrogating stance, we won't achieve a diverse culture, nor will we be able to build great leaders. We spend many hours a day with our work groups, and yet we know so little about each other. We have little connection and little humanity in our work lives, which all contribute to misunderstandings and ultimately diversity issues. People often cluster themselves into specialty groups as a way to find support, but, in reality, we all just want to be treated like individuals, and we want to grow.

My background is fairly diverse. I grew up as a first-gen-

> **The humanistic side of our business has suffered because of the fear of retaliation and litigation. The walls we have built to protect us also create an environment where it is difficult for people to bring out their best.**

eration American. My parents emigrated from Spain as young children, but they grew up in an enclave of other Spaniards. They spent most of their lives living in the United States, but you never would know it. Fifty families clustered together, living out a Spanish life in the United States. They all inter-married; they all were fully immersed in Spanish culture so it wasn't until my generation came along that we actually ventured outside of the Spanish community. I grew up in a Spanish-speaking household where it was normal to have four parents since our grandparents lived with us. Having our grandparents live with us was not unusual for the Spanish culture. All of this happened in New York, in rural Long Island. Ironically, every time I tell people that I am from New York and of Spanish descent, people immediately think of me as someone who grew up in the city, living perhaps in Brooklyn or Queens with Puerto Rican friends and neighbors. In reality, I grew up in rural Long Island amongst potato farms and beaches. My high school graduating class had about a hundred kids in it, and I was never considered as anything but a Caucasian from Spain. This is not what people think of when they meet me for a first time or even after fifteen years of working with me.

> **Great leaders open their eyes and are as open as humanly possible to see people as they present themselves, not based on their internal biases or previous expectations.**

When I traveled and lived more in the Southwest and in Texas, I was immediately considered Mexican. I never even knew what a taco was growing up in New York. Paella, yes. Taco, no! And yet people never asked the questions, never understood my orientation. Instead they lumped me into "Hispanic" with all of their own interpretations about what this meant for them. I am very Spanish with much cultural pride for my family upbringing and cultural origin, but not once have I been asked about my background. Can I connect and relate to other "Hispanic" groups? Certainly yes. But perhaps people felt as though it was taboo to say, "Tell me about your Hispanic heritage." I bet a large percentage of people would think it is taboo to ask or maybe they are just too unknowledgeable about different cultures. Either way, I would say that it isn't something they would venture to ask.

I have a Black woman colleague/friend who has had similar frustrations. She is from Jamaica and has some significant cultural differences with southern African-Americans, but nobody would ever ask her where she was from.

We have become fearful about asking people who they are. We have lost our humanity. Where is the respect for the individual? All of this is needed if we are to grow great leaders. The way our corporate environments are today doesn't allow us to build a diverse culture one person at a time, and this also doesn't foster great leadership. I really don't appreciate being lumped into this broad generic "Hispanic" category, but that is how it is today. Great leaders open their eyes and are as open as humanly possible to see people as they present themselves, not based on their internal biases or previous expectations. This is hard stuff to master, but building great leadership requires the love of people and the interest and curiosity to know the inner workings of people.

> All people, regardless of the role they play in an organization or their race, gender, age or ethnicity, want to be seen as the individuals they are and to bring their unique strengths to the table. They all want to contribute.

All people, regardless of the role they play in an organization or their race, gender, age or ethnicity, want to be seen as the individuals they are and to bring their unique strengths to the table. They all want to contribute. Or in Don's words "They want to do their best work."

Imagination is more important than knowledge. Knowledge is limited. Imagination encircles the world.

—Albert Einstein

CHAPTER 6

Building Connections for
an Innovative Culture

When you study companies that have great innovative cultures where magic happens and people are energized about being there, great leadership is usually present. Having great leaders also means that you probably have a fairly diverse environment, where respect flows both ways between people. People are usually free to be themselves and the culture doesn't impose on them to fit into a specific mold. Great leaders recognize the importance of imagination and that a certain climate and environment is needed to foster imagination. An Innovative Culture needs both great leaders and great diversity where our imaginations can be set free.

You need trust, vulnerability and curiosity to build great leadership and you need great leadership to encourage diversity and an innovative culture, but who wants to step out there and be vulnerable?

At its core, innovation is about risk-taking and dreaming about "what if" and the possibilities of something different and something new. Imagination, not knowledge, is the catalyst for innovation. You can't achieve innovation without trust and without vulnerability. It seems like a "catch 22." You need trust, vulnerability and curiosity to build great leadership and you need great leadership to encourage diversity and an innovative culture, but who wants to step out there and be vulnerable?

A friend and fellow speaker, colleague Karen McCullough, says, "Change is good. You go first." The same is true for putting ourselves out there and opening up and being real and vulnerable. It not only takes courage, but we need to confront some real fears. We always want to say that change starts at the top. It is easy not to assume responsibility. No matter where you sit in the organization, the top seems to be further up than you. So what ends up happening is that we all end up waiting for someone else to begin. Yet it all starts with each and every one of us.

Take baby steps and open up to your small work groups by telling them your own personal stories so that they understand your core values. Then take it a step further and open up to a fellow colleague or a superior. You will be surprised how far genuine interest in someone will take you.

> It does take the collective effort of many to change a culture. Each and every person needs to step outside and be real to themselves and others in order to create a culture that is based on great leadership and fosters diversity of thinking and innovation.

It does take the collective effort of many to change a culture. Each and every person needs to step outside and be real to themselves and others in order to create a culture that is based on great leadership and fosters diversity of thinking and innovation. What I found across companies was that when they wanted to innovate, their first steps were focused on setting up innovation processes and models. While it is important to capture innovative ideas and to guide them down a funnel towards in-market execution, I was always baffled as to why they would start there. It is truly putting the cart before the horse.

The momentum of innovation does not start with a model or process, it starts with a culture. It is often these intangible areas like culture and engagement that are the spirit behind innovation. So the essential elements of connection that drive leadership are also the connection needed to foster creativity, imagination and innovation.

Having come through the ranks of marketing where we are known to be of the creative ilk, one thing that is clear about creativity is that one needs to feel safe and free to be "off the wall" in order to find innovative ideas where our imaginations are set free. Often times, people want to harness innovation too early on; there truly are no bad ideas when it comes to imagination. In fact, the wackier the better. But how many times do we allow people in a corporate setting to be wacky and off the wall? Certainly not often enough.

> One way to start is by creating an environment where it is believed that you can be an individual and that we can break free of the consensus mind set. In organizations where the collective mind set is powerful, it is hard for an individual to stand apart. It takes a great deal of effort and courage to be different. This is where leadership needs to set a tone of acceptance and openness.

One way to start is by creating an environment where it is believed that you can be an individual and that we can break free of the consensus mind set. In organizations where the collective mind set is powerful, it is hard for an individual to stand apart. It takes a great deal of effort and courage to be different. As Albert Einstein once said, "Any fool can make things bigger, more complex, and more violent. It takes a touch of genius—and a lot of courage—to move in the opposite direction." This is where leadership needs to set a tone of acceptance and openness. While it might seem overly simplistic, it is the little actions, the little comments and the little ways in which things are handled that set the tone for an organization. This is where vulnerability comes in. When we are vulnerable, we are free to be ourselves. When leaders free themselves to be who they are, they give permission to others to do the same.

I recently read in Judith E. Glaser's book, *The DNA of Leadership,* that recent studies analyzing the differences in men and women show that men are actually threatened in social situations but women find more solace and comfort in social situations. This conclusion concerned me. Our business environments and corporate cultures are still male-dominated, particularly at the higher levels. The organization Catalyst tracks and monitors the numbers of women in leadership roles across organizations large and small, and they have recently reported a flattening in the number of women in leadership roles. Despite the advances in corporate businesses, women are still not at representative levels in leadership roles.

> When we let others see the truth in us, then we have more integrity and others are willing to trust us more.

When I speak about opening up and becoming vulnerable in social settings as a way to encourage our associates to do the same, it is clear that this is not a strength that we have in our male-centered corporate environments. This is not intended to be a slam on men. To the contrary, if men are more threatened in social situations, and they are the ones who lead our corporate cultures, then it is going to take a great deal of hard work to help men feel safe in opening up and sharing their personal stories in a group setting. We want innovation and we want creativity to flow in our companies. In my own situation, I found more power when I opened up. This is contrary to what most people would think to be true. It is one of those ironic twists of human nature. When we let others see the truth in us, then we have more integrity, and others are willing to trust us more. If your perception is that in hiding your vulnerabilities, you are giving off an image of strength, forget it! People, like children, are able to sniff that out. We intuitively know when we have the full, real deal in front of us or a shell-of-a-person who shows up telling us to give it our all. They see right through it.

Your company culture may support the belief that you need to be suspicious of others; and therefore, it would seem risky to open up and share yourself. Remember that each time you don't open up you are locking up your organization. It takes one person at a time to unlock or change a culture. One person does not hold the keys. You need to help set people free so that they can do their best and bring their best each and every day.

> Mary spoke from her heart to us that day, and she told us about choices and how each choice has its joy and its implications. I wanted more. I wanted to hear about her journey and her struggles.

One time at The Coca-Cola Company, we had a women's executive leadership forum. There was a relatively small group of women leaders present, perhaps fifty or so. Mary, one of our then highest ranking female executives spoke to us. Mary is an awesome business person and marketing professional. I had always looked up to her, and I was exceedingly proud to have such a brilliant and smart woman in such an important position at the company. Mary spoke from her heart to us that day, and she told us about choices and how each choice has its joy and its implications. I wanted more. I wanted to hear about her journey and her struggles. I was so motivated and inspired that I wrote her a heartfelt letter telling her that she had the power to set many of us free by sharing her story. I knew it was tough for her. Her armor was well-developed. I understood, because I had mine, too. But I know that she listened. I know in my heart that she heard me and knew exactly what I meant. Mary, fortunately and unfortunately, later resigned from the company. Fortunately, because I think she did it for herself and for her life, and unfortunately, because the women at The Coca-Cola Company needed her. She could have helped many of us to share our stories. An innovative culture allows all people to have a voice.

Great ideas come from everywhere. If your "leadership style" is one of command and control, then achieving an innovative culture would be difficult to create. Again, parenting is a great teacher for this example. When a child isn't free to explore because the rules are too tight and the reins are not loose enough, that child ultimately rebels and doesn't learn how to fully contribute to his or her brilliance. The child needs guidance and guardrails, but they need to be free to mess up. Creativity is messy. It is in the imperfection of chaos that creativity can actually flourish and innovative ideas will surface. If you were to ever interview an artist, or if you have an artistic interest, you would understand that you can't schedule creativity. You can't say, "Okay, today from 1-3 p.m., I am going to be creative and make some art. Now get to it."

Creativity is not something you can command. Ask a couple who is trying to conceive. The ultimate creation of pregnancy is also mysterious and happens with its own rhythm and way. Creativity is spontaneous. It flows through people, and you need to foster its development by encouraging an environment where people can be themselves. You have to create an environment that empowers creativity. An environment that is safe to explore and fail.

I love to see companies where people are encouraged to create their own unique work space environments. The Internet inspired a lot of this new organizational thinking. The Yahoos and Googles of the world live and die on their innovations and creativity. This is one area of business where people are encouraged to be themselves and their creativity is let loose. Jeans and flip flop-clad employees bring their dogs to work. Here, hierarchy is minimized and people don't put on airs about who they are.

Companies need to stand out from all of the competition. People's imaginations are limitless; ideas are what will set us apart. Great ideas come from messiness and from a level of acceptance that only great leadership can foster. A secure leader isn't threatened by an individual who might be uncommon or even strange. This leader knows how to find their brilliance and use it to the advantage of the whole. Stand up and be the leader that you can be, regardless of where you sit in an organization. Your impact makes a difference to you and your people!

> **Companies need to stand out from all of the competition. People's imaginations are limitless; ideas are what will set us apart. Great ideas come from messiness and from a level of acceptance that only great leadership can foster.**

PART II
THE SEVEN ESSENTIAL LEADERSHIP INSIGHTS

Leadership is the art of getting someone else to do something you want done because he wants to do it.

—Dwight D. Eisenhower

PART II

The Seven Essential Leadership Insights

The seven essential insights for leadership that I have developed are the basis of my curriculum to help people embody leadership as a life practice for success. These insights have been inspired by the experiences and challenges I faced in my more than twenty years of corporate business experience coupled with late-life parenting. These insights are also based in my never-ending journey of learning how to help unleash another human's greatest gifts and potential, which is my purpose as a parent and a leader. These insights have also allowed me to get more out of my life, both at work and at home.

These insights are intended to help bring a balance between business management and leadership that our businesses so desperately need.

I believe that these essential leadership insights will provide you with some inspiration to complement your own journey to become a more effective leader. These insights also illuminate the fact that when you allow others to fulfill their dreams, you inherently achieve your own dreams through them. This is the amazing mystery of leadership. In setting others free to be who they are, they in turn give you what you want and need. I love the quote by Dwight D. Eisenhower because it gives the full picture. As you help others realize their potential, they help you. Everyone grows and gets what they need and want. What a great win-win!

My hope is to inspire you through my openness and my stories. My deepest desire is to have these insights help you, and ultimately your organization, to change your vantage point so that you can be the type of leader who can change your work environment and bring more meaning and importance to your work life.

These insights are intended to help bring a balance between business management and leadership that our businesses so desperately need. The goal is to have more productive, fulfilled, creative and inspired people generating long-term results. Each of these insights is more fully explained in its own section. It is important to draw on your own personal experiences to help you crystallize what these insights look like, as well as feel like, when they are in practice.

The first step is to become aware of your actions and behavior. You will learn how to gradually shift your paradigm for a more effective change in your approach. Remember that I can't teach you to be a better leader, but you can learn to be a better leader. Spend time getting to know yourself. Great leadership starts with a keen sense of self-awareness. But as General Norman Schwarzkopf said, "When asked to lead, take charge." Take charge in a responsible, caring way. Step into leadership fully committed and connected.

If you judge people, you have no time to love them.

—Mother Theresa

INSIGHT 1

Believe and Let Go

How we believe in people sets the tone for the type of leader we are. Believing that people can do the right thing. Believing that associates can make the right choices. Believing that someone may have a better answer. Believing that a co-worker may know more. Believing is what allows us to let go and get the best out of people. When we believe and let go, we let others confront their own abilities or inabilities. When we let go, we give people the opportunity to ask for help and guidance. When we let go, we allow others to learn what works for them. My good friend and colleague, Tom, told me that parenting is a never-ending process of "letting go." I love that because that is what leadership is also about. We need to "let go" for people to soar to their greatest heights. In order to do this, we must *believe* in them.

> When we believe and let go, we let others confront their own abilities or inabilities. When we let go, we give people the opportunity to ask for help and guidance.

The inverse of believing is doubting. When we doubt others, what we really are saying is that we only value them for what they can do for us. We value them for what their actions say about us. When we doubt others, we are telling them that our way is the only way. When we doubt others, we limit them, and we limit ourselves. This is a very self-centered approach. We give far too much credit to ourselves and none to the other individual.

When we brought home our daughter from Russia, she was developmentally delayed by about three to four months. This was to be expected because she had spent the first eleven months of her life in an orphanage where mental and physical stimulation were very limited. She was delayed with her fine and gross motor skills as well as her social interacting skills. Lewis and I worked hard at understanding her needs and doing our very best to give her what she needed; we did what every loving parent does every day. We saw our child's needs, and we found ways to fill them; however, our daughter, Leila, did the work. She worked hard at catching up. She was the one who asked me to walk up and down the cracked sidewalk a zillion times until she could master it on her own. She was a trooper when she trusted our decision to allow her loving nanny, Gloria, to care for her. She took risks within the environment we provided her. People give us accolades about how far she has come and how she really is a "normal" three year old who has warmed up to a broader and broader circle of people and is chatting up a storm. In reality, we did nothing more, or nothing less, than any other

> **We often don't ever give people the credit they deserve. When we believe in them, we give them the credit they deserve. We can value someone so much by simply recognizing the road they have traveled.**

parent would have done. We never forget all the work that our little Leila did to become the amazing being that she is!

We often don't give people the credit they deserve. When we believe in them, we give them the credit they deserve. We can value someone so much by simply recognizing the road they have traveled. The experiences they have garnered and the things they bring to bear in new and challenging situations is unique. Each of our roads is so different.

When I was starting up the new business venture for Minute Maid and we began to gain momentum, I was given the opportunity to expand my team. I brought on Allison, a bright Stanford graduate with an MBA from the University of Texas at Austin. She was one smart cookie, but she was very green. She had some experience in New York working for the David Letterman show, but her brand marketing skills weren't particularly developed. She had learned the theory from some great training at the University of Texas and some case study application, but she had little to no real-world experience. Allison stepped into an environment that was a bit like a start up. We had lots of expectations and numbers to meet, but we had no people or little support to get it done. I believed in Allison's ability to figure things out, so I gave her free rein. There were times when Allison would come to me a bit nervous and say, "You know I don't want to screw up, Laura. I am afraid that I don't know what I don't know." All I could say to her was, "Don't worry; I won't let you mess up

> Fundamentally, I was afraid that someone would mess something up and I would be the one holding the bag. I found that it often became a self-fulfilling prophecy. The more I doubted, the more folks messed up and didn't give their best.

big." I gave her enough rope with guidance so that she could flourish and do well. I believed in her abilities to figure things out. I also believed and trusted her judgment in raising the red flags when she needed to.

I have never been disappointed when I believed in people. In fact, I have been amazed more often than not when I let go. But I can't say that I always heeded this advice. In fact, there was a time in my career, especially at the beginning when I was just learning the skills of leading people, that I was doubtful that people could ever be able to do what I was able to do. My way was the best way; no one could do it better. Fundamentally, I was afraid that someone would mess something up and I would be the one holding the bag. I found that it often became a self-fulfilling prophecy. The more I doubted, the more folks messed up and didn't give their best. In return, my doubt was validated and reaffirmed, so I kept on doubting. Early on, I became that micro-managing, controlling boss who couldn't let anyone do their job because no one could do it quite like I could. Operating from this position is really quite exhausting. I thought there had to be a better way. I finally realized that I needed to delegate, to let go. Doing that, I had to believe that people would come through.

I had a mentor who told me that other people's 100 percent will always be your 80 percent and that you needed to start getting comfortable with 80 percent. I fought that for some time since I have always been an overachiever. With time, I realized that 80 percent quickly became 100 percent plus when I gave people the space they needed and my belief in them. When we approach people with doubt, they shut down. They don't really want to give you what they've got unless they want to prove you wrong. Even then, you probably wouldn't be able to believe in them if you are stuck in a doubtful stance.

Sometimes believing in someone is most difficult when that someone is especially different from us. This is when doubt gets coupled with suspicion. In these circumstances, we want the "credentials" that will prove to us that this person is worth believing. While credentials are clearly important in many aspects of our lives, relying exclusively on credentials can cause us to miss some true gifts in people that are often the result of their life or work experiences. Our culture thrives on proving "expert" status. Fortunately, I have found that some of this is being challenged in our culture as more and more people are venturing into second and third careers by leveraging their experiences rather than getting that second or third master's degree. Also, the new millennial generation is challenging the status quo. They are now redefining success on their terms. I find this refreshing since my belief is that there are few times in our lives where we are really "starting from scratch."

> **Sometimes believing in someone is most difficult when that someone is especially different from us. This is when doubt gets coupled with suspicion.**

When I ventured into my second career as an author, speaker and consultant, many folks, including myself at times, froze with fear. How will you live? You are going to write and speak on leadership? What are your qualifications to do that? The answers were obvious. I wasn't twenty years old and just starting out. I had more than twenty years of invaluable experience to share. I was a leader for many years. I managed large pieces of business and teams of people. I was not starting all over. Each of us has a wealth of talent that we amass, and we should never minimize it in ourselves or in others. We never are starting from scratch. Neither are the folks working for you. They have insights you probably can't even fathom because their experiences have naturally been different from yours!

A quick personal story comes to mind here. As my husband and I ventured down the adoption path, we bought many books to help us prepare for the unexpected and unknown. One book in particular struck a chord with me, and I asked my husband, who is an engineer, to read it. He picked up the book, read the front and back cover and said, "Where are this woman's credentials? What makes her an expert on this topic of adoption?" He wanted to see something like Ph.D., International Adoption, after her name. While his question was a valid one, so was my response. "Her credentials are based on her experience; this book is based on her personal journey into adoption." He replied, "Well, why should I listen to it? She's no expert in the area of adoption."

> Hierarchy can be a proxy for the "credentials" we seek to validate who we should and shouldn't believe. When we only believe in those with a title and we don't listen to those without one, our ability to be a great leader has fallen short.

I realized that maybe he was looking for a cross section of perspectives, a broader view than just one experience. I respected that. I, on the other hand, felt that her experience was valuable. This exchange helped me to see how ingrained our culture is in having experts and proving credentials. There were, in fact, books that provided us with the statistics and the facts related to adoption, information we also were seeking, but her book provided us with a live case study that gave us some real insight.

I am not suggesting that we eliminate the need for credentials or experts. You certainly wouldn't want to schedule orthopedic surgery with someone who didn't have a degree in medicine, a specialty in orthopedics, and hundreds of operations under his/her belt. However, when we are exclusively skewed toward valuing people solely for their credentials, then we might miss a great deal of brilliance and experience that may not have the stripes and stars to validate their "opinions." Clearly we make our own choices about whom we listen to and whom we dismiss, but it is important to be aware which side of the equation you are on at all times. Just because you are a director, beware if you don't listen to administrative assistants or managers on your team. Hierarchy can be a proxy for the "credentials" we seek to validate who we should and shouldn't believe. When we only believe in those with a title and we don't listen to those without one, our ability to be a great leader is diminished.

Start believing in the power of people and begin to let go and you will see that the best will come your way. This approach is optimistic. You are assuming that people will bring their best to the table rather than assuming that they won't or that they need to *prove it* to you first.

Think about how you might react to someone who is waiting for you to prove your worth. You know that you are on ground zero and that what you produce today will dictate your future value. Or you really need to prove your best before you receive any respect. It really feels like "What have you done for me lately?" There is no inherent belief in you and what you can bring to bear. Under this approach, it will be difficult to bring out the very best in someone, and it is an approach that promotes burnout. They are pushing that boulder up the hill each day,

> Think about how you might react to someone who is waiting for you to prove your worth. You know that you are on ground zero and that what you produce today will dictate your future value. Or you really need to prove your best before you receive any respect. It really feels like "What have you done for me lately?"

perhaps reaching the top by the end of the day. At the start of each new day, they find themselves once again at the bottom. They may show you their best, but over time they will burn out.

We can also borrow from parenting here. What do we provide our children? Unconditional love. When a child ventures out into the world, we know that he or she eventually will confront difficulties with other children and other situations. We expect them to do their best and to deal with these difficulties in a manner that is based on the family's belief system and values. We watch and coach them, expecting them to put forth their best effort. When they don't, we correct them and we guide them. But all of the time, we expect them to bring their best. They usually live up to that expectation. When you expect the best, you get the best. If we did the opposite, and expected them to screw up or not to employ what they have learned, you may bet with nearly 100 percent accuracy that this child will not successfully bring their best to every situation.

> He respected my position, the fact that I had gotten to where I was for a reason, and that I had been contributing to the company for some time. That alone had value for him. He didn't need to see proof that I was smart. He assumed that I was.

At the end of the day, our people are just big children who want to be recognized for their unique perspectives and contributions. Valuing them for what they bring to the table is a first priority for leadership.

My story about Don is relevant here. One of the reasons I clearly put him on my "only" list of leaders was that he fundamentally believed, without having to really know, that I was capable. He respected my position, the fact that I had gotten to where I was for a reason, and that I had been contributing to the company for some time. That alone had value for him. He didn't need to see proof that I was smart. He assumed that I was.

On the other hand, I once had a boss who was convinced that I didn't belong where I was, and he needed me to prove my worth on a daily basis. Perhaps I did things differently than he would have done it. Perhaps he didn't like my way of working. I know we had different ways of approaching things based on our orientations. This boss' interactions with me supported his beliefs and with every interaction he looked for my next mistake.

You can see how this orientation can have dramatically different outcomes. A "development" discussion with Don would come from a supportive and productive stance, one in which any associate would strive to put their best foot forward. A "development" discussion with the latter boss would amount to a feeling that he was trying to find what else was wrong. A person's inherent value and experience should be enough "proof" for any leader.

Do you believe in your associates? Do you let go and allow them to do brilliant work?

I have no special talent. I am only passionately curious.

—Albert Einstein

INSIGHT 2

Be Curious and See Everyone

Just like leadership is similar to parenting, teams can be a lot like families. If you came from a family where your parents had "favorites," you can see how this style of management could be a recipe for disaster. Having favorites at home and in the work environment usually breeds a situation that is counter to the goals that a true leader, or great parent, seeks. Having favorites is one way of saying that we are only willing to "see" certain types of individuals.

In Insight 1, Believe and Let Go, one of the reasons we might give "air time" to one person and not to another is because of the credentials that come with position and title. In Insight 2, Be Curious and See Everyone, we might exclude someone simply because we are no longer curious about that person. We have decided that we know all there is to know about them, and we no longer need to hear their point of view. We have written them off. When this happens, not only does this person notice, but so does the entire organization. What is being said to the organization, intentionally or not, is that only certain characteristics and ways of being will be listened to in this organization. The one that has been cast out is showing unfavorable and unacceptable ways. This can be an effective technique to show an organization what isn't acceptable when it is consciously done. However, the reality is that leaders often do this with no awareness that they are doing it. They are merely "seeing" or listening to those who are more in line with their way of thinking.

This is unfortunately very common. The implications are disastrous, because it informs people that only certain criteria will get you into the club. When a leader does this, greater tolerance is required and a bigger lens is needed so that the full team can be viewed and heard, not just certain players. Breeding an exclusive environment often leaves the outsiders with little ability to grow or even contribute. Even the insiders don't grow because they aren't challenged. The end result is that everyone loses. This environment breeds a "team" that can't win for the long haul.

> **Breeding an exclusive environment often leaves the outsiders with little ability to grow or even contribute. Even the insiders don't grow because they aren't challenged. The end result is that everyone loses.**

Curiosity is central to this insight, because curiosity allows us to see people in a new light. As Einstein says in the quote at the beginning of this section, talent is secondary to curiosity. When we are curious, we seek first to understand others and situations, which is Stephen Covey's fifth habit in *The 7 Habits of Highly Effective People*. This allows a broader set of people to have a place. As a leader, you need to be curious about everyone on the team, even if they are just warming the bench.

I love watching children be curious because adults seem to have lost so much of this trait. I am not sure at what point we think we have it all figured out and from that point forward, we are simply trying to validate our point of view. The more we can suspend judgment and remain open to people, the more we can allow curiosity to flourish within us.

This always brings up a personal story for me. When we were in the process of adopting our daughter and we had just brought her home, the question most asked of us was how we had selected her. I found this question very intriguing. My daughter has blonde curly hair and blue eyes. I guess I look more like her nanny than I do her Mom. The reason I believe this question was so commonly asked is because we, as humans, find comfort in having like people around us. It is a well-known fact that we are more likely to select others who resemble ourselves than not. We have known that differences can make us uncomfortable. Differences can challenge our reality. The fact is that my daughter is adopted. She looks different because she doesn't share my or my husband's DNA. I am obviously okay with that. Our choice was that she didn't have to look like us. Another couple may make another choice because it might be really important to them that there be some resemblance. My point in bringing this story up is not to say that our way was the only way, but to point out how salient this natural tendency is.

> **As a leader, you need to be curious about everyone on the team, even if they are just warming the bench.**

As adults, we don't necessarily like to be curious because we have developed an uncanny ability to be self-centered. We like to be listened to more than we like listening to others. We want our point of view to be understood before we understand others. Curiosity takes us outside of ourselves. Being curious about someone means that we are investing in another person. We are interested in learning about them. Being curious shows that you value the other person and you value their perspectives and ideas.

As for our daughter, the truth is that we didn't actively pick her out of a group of orphans; adoption doesn't work that way. Having a biological child doesn't quite work that way, either. Fate gave us exactly what we asked for: an amazing, healthy little girl. Parenting teaches a great deal about being curious. After all, every child comes chock-full of personality and perspectives worth exploring. If you let them, they will guide you and teach you how to effectively work with them. I learned this lesson by first respecting and acknowledging that my daughter is an independent being.

> **We are interested in learning about them. Being curious shows that you value the other person and you value their perspectives and ideas.**

Too often parents make the same mistake that leaders make. They don't recognize and respect the individual before them. Leaders and parents believe "I know all that you are going to learn." Instead, if you start to believe and practice that you are here to support and serve, you become a lot more curious about their wants and needs. You don't have to put forth your lessons. Your student will seek them. It also means that you don't impose your reality or your will on others. When we impose our reality or our will onto others, there isn't enough room for their own. So we rob them of their potential and they can't ever perform to their fullest capability.

> **When we impose our reality or our will onto others, there isn't enough room for their own. So we rob them of their potential and they can't ever perform to their fullest capability.**

In business today, there is a growing need for diversity. Diversity of thought, diversity of perspective, and leveraging diversity to make a difference. We know that in the ever-complex and ultra-competitive environments in which we operate, sameness won't lead us to robustness, sustainable growth or innovation. Differences make a difference, and we need to remind ourselves to be curious about others. It is curiosity that helps to see that others might have a different viewpoint that will help us solve a problem.

I like to tell a story of when my husband and I were traveling from Atlanta to Houston, where we had spent a weekend at a friend's home. We happened to sit next to a very smelly, homeless-looking guy in his mid-forties who, quite frankly, looked a bit scary to me. He looked like he hadn't shaved or bathed in about two weeks. We sat down doing the usual things that people do when they don't want to engage with strangers on an airplane. We were all staring straight ahead, or we buried our noses in our books and magazines. I fortunately had the window seat, but my poor husband, who had offered to take the middle seat, had to sit right next to this guy for the next two hours. We took off, and it looked like we were going to have a quiet flight. All of a sudden, my husband broke the silence and turned to the smelly guy and asked, "Is Houston home for you, or will you just be visiting?" I couldn't believe my ears. Here was my husband, the engineer, an introvert, starting a dialogue with a strange guy who looked like he beat his wife. I decided that I was going to keep my nose buried and not be a part of the conversation. I figured it would soon fizzle, and we would all be silent again. Half an hour into it, I overheard something that caught my attention: "I am really into scuba diving, too. Did you like the shark diving off of the coast of Africa?"

I was puzzled. Lewis nudged me and said, "Laura, meet Dr. Jones. He is an ophthalmologist, and he is familiar with

Leila's diagnosis of Strabismus." The doctor/ex-wife beater said, "I was telling Lewis that Strabismus in children is not really that uncommon, so I wouldn't worry too much about your daughter. The operation is quite simple."

The old saying, "You can't judge a book by its cover" hit me solidly over the head. I felt terribly ignorant for pre-judging this person. But what I really learned in that moment is how curiosity, in this case Lewis' curiosity to engage in dialogue, led to a change in our perspective. Suddenly, this person had something to add to a particularly difficult situation we were experiencing with our daughter. It turned out that the doctor had just gotten back from a two week hunting trip in the remote wilderness with his older son and had not shaved or showered in two weeks.

I was really wrong. I had judged too quickly. When we judge, we certainly lose the ability to be curious. We don't have to be curious with every stranger we meet; however, we need to be curious about our employees and colleagues who work with us day-in and day-out.

We can't be curious if we think we already know everything there is to know. We need to have the ability to open up our lens to those we would normally keep out of our view. In our fast-paced, insecure world, we have lost some of our curiosity for others. This insight goes hand in hand with the first one, because we first have to see the inherent value of a person before we are likely to seek information about that individual. When we show curiosity toward others, it also brings out the best in people.

> We can't be curious if we think we already know everything. We need to have the ability to open up our lens to those we would normally keep out of our view. In our fast-paced, insecure world, we have lost some of our curiosity for others.

They feel valued and respected for their individuality. No matter what race, gender, ethnicity or age a person is, they still want to be seen and heard for the individual they are.

Inclusivity fosters great teamwork. Team members know their roles; they get rotated in and everyone knows it's a team sport. They even self-select and prioritize for you. It is amazing to watch how they recognize where their natural strengths are. They self-regulate and build trust amongst each other.

When a leader has a favorite or favorite type, the environment is closed. People spend more time feeling bad and complaining than actually contributing. This also breeds resentment amongst the team. Playing favorites is emotionally immature behavior from a leader, but it happens all the time.

Why does it happen? Because we are all pressed for time and we have a big deadline impending or we need to pull together a presentation quickly. We know that if we give it to Emily instead of Bill that it'll be easier for us. Emily gets it. She knows exactly how I think, and I know that I won't need to rework it again and again. So I keep going to Emily. In meetings when Emily speaks, I listen. When others offer their perspectives, I gloss over and on to the next. These behaviors impact our ability to be effective leaders. Like parents, we need to be sensitive to the reactions of others as we engage with each other. It is hard work, but it is the work of a true leader.

Like Mike said to me as we left for Russia to adopt our daughter, "Dealing with the kids takes time." The same is true with employees. You can ignore an employee, believing that you have more important things to do, like get that new product packaging approved, or look at some TV storyboards, or attend a meeting. In the long run, you will suffer if you don't take the time. If you lead people, they should be your highest priority. It does take time, but it is time well invested.

Having favorites has a poisonous impact on the organization. It ultimately will drive good talent away. Even those favorites may become an unfavored associate under another leader and others will retaliate. This also causes cliques within organizations where collaboration is not fostered. The impact can be so broad that you don't even see it. Make sure your actions match your words. You might say that you are treating everyone the same, but you inadvertently leave people off the list of key meetings. You frequently invite your favorite to present on your behalf. You pal around and go out to lunch with your favorite. All of this speaks volumes to the entire team.

Never show favoritism. Never forget you are a leader. Since it is only human that we may feel more comfortable with people like ourselves, it is critical to gain this awareness. This is not only disastrous for inclusivity, but playing favorites will crush creativity and any chance for great leadership. Remember, great leaders are curious about their people. Great leaders want all of their team members to be successful. A great leader works hard at building curiosity toward people they may not personally like. Fostering curiosity about your people can begin to move you away from having favorites.

> Never show favoritism. Never forget you are a leader. Since it is only human that we may feel more comfortable with people like ourselves, it is critical to gain this awareness.

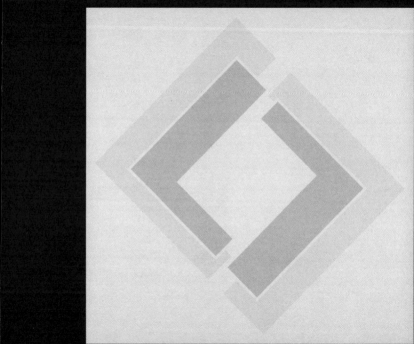

Leadership is practiced not so much in words as in actions.

—Harold S. Geneen

Be Receptive and Yield

My dad always got mad at me for "leading" when we would dance together. I grew up in an immigrant family where much of my Spanish heritage and culture was expressed by the music and dance of our roots. We were a musical family and dance accompanied much of our lives. I never took formal dance lessons, I just "felt" the music, observed, and got it. I never quite got the knack of "following" in dance. Quite frankly, as an independent, American-born, take-charge young woman, I wasn't sure if I liked the notion of the man "leading" and me following. We managed to dance our dance, but often I would break free and do my own thing. I never quite accomplished the elegant "two moving as one" dancing with my dad that my parents often demonstrated. It took

> I never realized that by yielding to my dad and receiving his direction, my mom was actually leading him! In fact, the women of the south would tell me, "You just have to make him believe he's the boss and only you know the reality: you are really the one leading him!"

me years to understand yielding and receiving as a way of leading. I had to move from New York to Atlanta, Georgia. You know the South, where women seem to be so soft spoken and demure, yet they *always* get their way! Steel Magnolias. I never realized that by yielding to my dad and receiving his direction, my mom was actually leading him! In fact, the women of the South would tell me, "You just have to make him believe he's the boss and only you know the reality: you are really the one leading him!"

This was a lesson I never forgot. This light clicked on again when I became a parent. When I yielded to my daughter's wishes and allowed her to satisfy her desires, she ultimately came around to do what I wanted her to do. When I insisted and rigidly attempted to force her to do what I wanted her to do, she invariably resisted. This resistance could go on for days. Directing rather than yielding goes back to some of my earlier myth busting. I had internalized a definition for leadership that only focused on the directing side of the coin. You could only lead by directing and having followers. This was my flawed view.

I believe that many people make this mistake, and even more, women in business make this grave mistake. They, like me, believe that you must be the one directing or "driving" at all times. When it comes to leadership, the opposite is true. The real leader is the one who yields and guides the energy of others. The leader is the quiet one who listens and asks the questions, not the one driving and giving the answers. This is a big mind shift for our

> They, like me, believe that you must be the one directing or "driving" at all times. When it comes to leadership, the opposite is true. The real leader is the one who yields and guides the energy of others. The leader is the quiet one who listens and asks the questions, not the one driving and giving the answers.

culture because the strong, domineering and directing type is often portrayed as the leader. I have found that it helps to think of leadership as a means of facilitating energy exchange. When you are the one pushing the agenda, it leaves little room for others' energy and will. As leaders, we want our people to have their own voice; we want to encourage energy flow between our associates. We want them to bring their own energy and will to the table. Our job as leaders is to subtly guide by being receptive and yielding to them.

The dance analogy is a great one because you can actually feel it in your body. You, too, can feel it in your body with a simple physical demonstration with a partner at home. I learned this technique from Gigi Sage of Power Connections. Stand back to back and interlock your arms with your partner. Both crouch down to a sitting position, so that you are leaning comfortably against each other with equal pressure. Take turns being the one to push with your legs (driving), while your partner is yielding or receiving and redirecting the energy. You will see that the push action is not the leading position; rather, it is the receptive position where we are best able to lead and guide the direction of others. This experience also reminds me of the palm tree.

Palm trees are the most receptive trees in nature. They bend to the winds like blades of grass. They clearly are found in tropical areas, where the winds are particularly strong. A rigid and hard tree would snap under the forces of the wind. When we lead from a receptive stance, we are like the palm tree; we bend and we flex to accommodate the energy of others around us.

I always try to encourage my daughter to do things "when she is ready." I may suggest something that she is highly resistant to, like getting her pajamas on before bedtime. All kids resist bedtime in general, and I think many parents have just accepted the fact that there will always be a nightly struggle with their children, particularly the younger ones. My technique works like a dream. I tell her in advance what my expectations are for her to get ready for bed. With sufficient time, I tell her that she needs to get her pajamas on when she is ready. I give her some defined parameters so that she doesn't keep "not being ready" all night long. This approach allows her to be in charge of her destiny, and I am being receptive to her needs.

In an office environment, it works wonders when we define problems without prescribing solutions. We allow people to come up with their own work plans within certain parameters of acceptability. This is yielding to them in a way that allows you, the leader, to guide the direction of their efforts. When we are so prescriptive and defined in our direction, we give little room for others to put in their two cents. Why bother having people work with you if you aren't going to allow them to contribute their own ideas and talent?

> When we are so prescriptive and defined in our direction, we give little room for others to put in their two cents. Why bother having people work with you if you aren't going to allow them to contribute their own ideas and talent?

One time in my career, I was absolutely certain about a particular direction we needed to take with the business. We were hoping to expand the Minute Maid brand beyond the refrigerated case by putting it in bottles and cans and distributing it across our bottling system. This required a particular economic model and required formula modifications to meet the economic and operational realities of the bottling system. I had done the analysis. I had the rationale that laid out the financial implications if we didn't take this direction and the upside if we did. My direct boss squashed my recommendation in no time. His reason was that he believed the formula change was not in keeping with the brand's history and promise. While his perspective was valid, it was rigid. With his rigidity, he was unwilling to bend to the needs of the business and to the future needs of the brand.

Many companies and brands can come to thresholds like this. With the changing times, we need to reinvent ourselves and our business models. These changes often require throwing out some old, worn out ideas that are no longer applicable to the new future we are seeking. Fortunately, my boss recognized the importance of this decision and opened up the discussion to the entire leadership team. He first demonstrated rigidity, but, after further thought, he also demonstrated a willingness to be receptive and yield to the consensus of the group. He exhibited great leadership skill in doing this because I know that his own personal belief was not in support of the direction we ultimately took. A true leader, like a palm tree, is receptive to the energies of the group, so much so that they are willing to yield to the decisions and directions of the team.

It doesn't take a hero to order men into battle. It takes a hero to be one of those men who goes into battle.

—General Norman Schwarzkopf

INSIGHT 4

Be Real and Serve

In parenting as in leadership, you can make the mistake of not serving your child/associate. You can make choices that work for you and make your day easier, but it might not be in their best interest. One thing that I realized when I became a parent is that I had spent almost my entire forty-four years making decisions in my life and in my work that were only in my best interest. Decisions were made for my ease and for my benefit as opposed to anyone else's. This became clear to me because it was through the experience of being a parent that the intention of my actions became more transparent.

> **Being a great leader, like being a great parent, takes effort, self-awareness and courage.**

A personal story can help illustrate this. When Leila first came home to Texas from Russia, I was anxious to show her to the world, particularly my family who lived in New York. I had read and been told that we really needed to limit her exposure to many people in the first six months because it can be quite overwhelming to a child whose entire world had been changed dramatically. Her world in an orphanage was quite limited and small, and now she had a much less controlled environment with many more strange faces and places. I was anxious for that time to pass, and, while I tried to respect it, I had every reason to believe that we didn't need the full six months. I also got a lot of pressure from my mom to visit. My family is the stereotypical Mediterranean family, where we have a ton of aunts and uncles who aren't really blood relatives. They all wanted to meet our daughter. I kept saying to my husband, "Oh come on, let's go to New York so that we can have the whole family meet Leila: she is ready." He finally said to me, "Whose best interest is that decision based on, yours or hers?" I guess Leila could really have cared less about New York and meeting more people. She probably just wanted to get better acquainted with us and her new home. Once again, my husband was right. I had been trying to make this decision based on my needs and wants, not hers. I was the one who wanted to show her off and interact with family and friends. We did wait until the six months were over, and it turned out that even then she wasn't fully ready. I spent a great deal of time inside with her because she was overwhelmed, and I ended up having not such a great time myself because she wasn't fully ready.

I realized then that in both parenting and in leadership, we often try to do things that serve our best interest, not our team's or our child's. Now going forward, I always ask myself "Who am I doing this for? Is it to serve Leila or myself?" I have gotten very clear about what her needs are and how I can help fill them and serve her.

When I returned to work after staying home with Leila, I used this question as a filter with my work associates and teams. I found that the clearer I got on what my intentions and motivations were, the clearer I was on my team's needs. The more that their needs were filled, the more they were able to contribute and perform to their best level. Now sometimes,

I must admit, we need to do things solely for our benefit. This is okay, as long as we are clear about our intention and that it doesn't negatively impact those whom we are responsible for. As you use this question as a filter, you will be amazed by how many things will fall aside as the wrong thing to do for your associates/ teams. Sometimes we are just trying to make things easy for ourselves without considering the impact these actions may have on others. Being a great leader, like being a great parent, takes effort, self-awareness and courage.

I love the symbol of an inverted pyramid to represent graphically the fact that we serve others when we are leaders in our lives. It also shows the beauty of starting with one, the single point of the pyramid, and showing the expansive and exponential impact that one can have on many. The inverted pyramid represents the opposite of a traditional hierarchy. Our corporate worlds are all based on a hierarchy best represented as a pyramid, where ultimately there is only one top dog and many soldiers "supporting" them. Most computer programs used in companies today from Microsoft Word to PowerPoint have ways to visually depict a hierarchical structure with the little boxes and lines. The concept is clear. As you go up the organization, the numbers are fewer and turfs are built with lots of little boxes "under" the leader.

The concept of servant leadership uses the inverted pyramid to depict the fact that the customer or consumer is ultimately the "top" of the organization. There is no business if we don't satisfy the customer's needs. James C. Hunter does an excellent job describing the concepts of servant leadership in *The Servant*. I wholeheartedly support the idea that as leaders, we are there to serve and support our teams. Far too often, we forget that it is our customers and end consumers whom we ultimately serve; they should always be at the top of any organization. Even if we are in business for ourselves, we still have consumers and customers whom we serve. They are whom we work for and they are at the *top.* Then come the many folks, the rank and file so to speak, who are closest to the customer. They are the next level who ensure that everything the organization is doing is supporting the customer. The last person in the inverted pyramid is the leader, who is there to serve the needs of the entire organization so that they can fulfill the customer's needs.

I do think, however, that we need traditional hierarchies to support some decision making. There are many instances where we need a final decision from a CEO. It is, however, important to achieve the balance of both the yin and the yang, incorporating the two sides of management and leadership. Traditional pyramid hierarchies support management decisions but inverted pyramid hierarchies support leadership. They go hand in hand but require different approaches and mindsets. When it is about leadership, the mindset must be about serving those who "work for you" as opposed to them serving you. If you aren't giving your team what they need, they won't be able to generate what you need. It's a quarterbacking mentality. You are there to support and guide the team to do the blocking and tackling. You can't quite point to the end line that they are striving for if you aren't in the game with them, standing side by side and seeing what they need to be successful. Continue to ask yourself the question: Whom am I doing this for? If your actions and behaviors are not serving your teams/associates/customers, then you should rethink your actions.

> Continue to ask yourself the question: Who am I doing this for? If your actions and behaviors are not serving your teams/associates/customers, then you should rethink your actions.

I used to have 8 a.m. Monday meetings with a team of

more than twenty folks when I was a director at The Coca-Cola Company. The meetings lasted two hours, and I found them to be incredibly helpful because it was my time to get updated on all of the projects that the team had going on. I also felt that it allowed the cross-functional team to hear the updates, too. I loved the debates and discussion that took place during these meetings since I used them as constructive training opportunities, and I thought it made us a stronger team. I began to hear lots of grumblings about the meetings, but never directly. The rumblings were mostly related to Monday mornings. It seemed that the team was not overly pleased with such an early start, particularly on Monday. At one of the meetings, I decided to open it up to the group to see if the meetings were working for them. When I asked for honest and open feedback, they slowly started out by saying things like, "Laura, maybe we can do it over lunch time? The 8 a.m. start is not ideal." I replied that most folks were already in at that time. I thought that there must be something else, and that the meeting time was not their main concern.

The further we dug in and the more they saw that I was not resistant to their input and ideas, I found out that the cross learning and updates were not as relevant to all the members of the team as I had thought. They each wanted to learn about what others were working on, but not once a week. They all had too much to get done, especially on Monday mornings, and the two-hour commitment wasn't productive for them. They suggested a rotating schedule so that each team could come in for their designated time. After their honest input, I realized why I had structured the meetings the way that I had. I had structured them for my benefit, not for theirs. With the learning and insight that they provided me, the way I had structured these meetings seemed silly. I realized that I had designed them with only me in mind. The meetings involved more than twenty people, and my objectives and needs were the only ones being met.

I thanked the folks who had the courage to come forward to alert me about the initial grumblings. I also thanked the team for its willingness to step up and come out with the real problem. None of this could have happened if I hadn't been in the field with them trying to serve them better. While this particular action didn't have them fully in mind, I am thankful that I was able to find out how to fix it in order to serve them. Can you imagine how many times we do things that aren't serving our teams and no one steps up to tell us? It is up to us as leaders to ensure that we keep our team's best interest in mind at all times, so that we are serving them and not ourselves.

> Can you imagine how many times we do things that aren't serving our teams and no one steps up to tell us? It is up to us as leaders to ensure that we keep our team's best interest in mind at all times, so that we are serving them and not ourselves.

Leadership does not depend on being right.

—Ivan Illich

INSIGHT 5

Be Humble and Keep Your Ego in Check

As managers and successful business leaders, you develop a habit of putting yourself in the center of things. After all, your entire life is spent competing. Getting great grades in high school to go to a great college. Competing with classmates for great grades. Competing for your first job opportunity. The story doesn't end here. It continues in the work place. You compete for promotions and to get results faster than the next guy.

When you are successful and you have many accomplishments, it's easy to give yourself a great deal of credit and to have built a sense of "I made it happen," "I drove those results," "I got it done." All of this can be true; great performance does require hard work, perseverance and drive. So it is understandable when we see hard-driving, results-oriented people who have overcome barriers, plowed through

> **The reality is that many rising stars in large organizations don't experience any, or enough, humiliation in their lives, either at work or at home. This is unfortunate. Humiliation can be a great teacher.**

walls and risen to the occasion promoted to higher and higher levels.

Yet, these attributes don't necessarily equate to being a great leader.

In fact, quite the opposite can be true. As Jim Collins identified in his research from *Good to Great,* a Level 5 leader is usually the antithesis to the ego-centered, charismatic, "high flash" leaders we often see. Level 5 leaders are humble. Webster defines humble as "not proud or haughty, not arrogant" and "offered in the spirit of deference or submission." These are things that don't usually go hand in hand with success. When we are successful, we can become proud and arrogant about our achievements; after all, not everyone gets to the top! What we often fail to understand is *how* people become humble. Humility is not a trait that is developed with success. Humility is often a gift that comes from being humiliated. Humiliation happens when one loses prestige and status, when we see that we are not superior to others, but that we are one and the same. Humiliation helps us see that we are all more alike than we are different. Humiliation allows us to empathize with others. Humiliation is a process in which the ego is put into its place.

The reality is that many rising stars in large organizations don't experience any, or enough, humiliation in their lives, either at work or at home. This is unfortunate. Humiliation can be a great teacher. I can tell you that I have experienced humiliation in my life on several occasions. I can't say that I would willingly sign up for it again. It is always a painful experience, but in retrospect I am grateful for these lessons because I am a better and more effective leader.

Back in 2003, my then-company was going through a major restructuring. I was running a multi-million dollar business that was on fire. It was growing both top and bottom lines, and I believed that when the restructuring was over I would be in a great position for another promotion. My colleague had been running a similar-sized piece of business on the top line, but it was probably one-third the size of my business when it came to the bottom line profits. His business had also been in decline for several years. The night before the restructuring was to be announced across the company, my boss called me to inform me that I had not been selected for the top job. With the restructuring, they were combining pieces of business, mine and that of my colleague, into one overall business. He was chosen to lead it. I was devastated. Not only was I not chosen, but I also had to report to my colleague. What made matters worse was that in the upcoming weeks, I was informed that 40 percent of my team had to be laid off. I was not involved in the final decision regarding which people had to go. My colleague, now boss, was the one who made all of these choices. I was not only devastated, but I was also humiliated because I had to go through with all of the layoffs as if they were my decision. Over the course of time, things continued to worsen. My team dwindled and the great business that I had worked so hard to build over the previous three years disappeared into a sea of other business units. I was so angry I couldn't see straight. The anger was a way for me to deal with the deep humiliation that I felt. I only came to understand this after a long period of being angry. It was a great lesson in humiliation and one that has made me a better leader than I ever could have been before this experience.

When you read the book, *Why CEOs Fail,* by David L. Dotlich and Peter C. Cairo, they define eleven behaviors that can derail your climb to the top. The first of eleven behaviors fits perfectly under this topic of humility, because it is the opposite of humility. The behavior is Arrogance: You're Right and Everybody Else is Wrong.

When I was going through my humiliating experience, I fell right into this behavior. How in the world could they have made this decision? I found I was spending a lot of time trying to prove that everyone who had anything to do with this decision was wrong and that I was right. After all, my business was humming. How could they be so blind? I wasn't accountable for other things that I may not have been doing well. I know that they had their reasons, even if I didn't agree with them. When I finally gave up trying to be right, I was able to deal with what was done and to dig deep into understanding what I wanted. I started to focus on the solution instead of trying to fix the problem.

While we know that self-confidence is an important attribute for all leaders and is a good thing, you get arrogant behavior when it is taken to the extreme and becomes ego-centricity. The authors of *Why CEO's Fail* speak about how arrogance is blinding. We get so caught up in being right all of the time that we believe that we are infallible. We think that we could never be wrong, thus we never are accountable. Power, prestige and success can breed this in leaders. The reality is that leaders like me who teetered toward the arrogant side will naturally come in contact with a humiliating experience to enlighten us. When leaders are arrogant, no one wants to work with them because they are always right, and no one's ideas or opinions matter. Humble people want to listen to others because they don't believe that they have all the answers. They also don't place themselves in the center of things; people with inflated egos do. The ego-centered, arrogant leader doesn't allow others to have a voice. So where are you on this continuum? Do you find that you are right more than you are ever wrong?

> While we know that self confidence is an important attribute for all leaders and is a good thing, you get arrogant behavior when it is taken to the extreme and becomes ego-centricity.

Do you find that you are always arguing your point, that you don't allow the opinions of others to be heard?

What parenting did for me was to take me out of my self-centeredness. When we are arrogant, we are the center of our own universe. Having children is a humbling experience. After thinking that I was in control of everything, I suddenly found myself in an environment where I knew absolutely nothing. According to Mike, and to some degree according to my beliefs, all of my prior training wasn't going to help me. I was in deep trouble. I had to accept that I was fallible and that I was going to make mistakes. I realized that I needed to learn how to be a great parent.

When leaders stop making mistakes, or believe that they are incapable of making mistakes, you know that they have tipped to the arrogant side. Great leaders don't have to be right all of the time. In fact, they want to be reminded how little they know in the face of a great team. A humble leader knows they can't be right all the time.

> **When leaders stop making mistakes, or believe that they are incapable of making mistakes, you know that they have tipped to the arrogant side. Great leaders don't have to be right all of the time. In fact, they want to be reminded how little they know in the face of a great team.**

What is your humbling opportunity? I can assure you that there are plenty of opportunities for them to surface in your life, but an arrogant person can also shirk them. Arrogance is so blinding that it doesn't see accountability. When I was humbled, I took the opportunity to work through the anger and to go deeper into understanding what really went wrong. I realized that my leadership sphere of influence needed to be broader and deeper. I was too focused on my piece of the business and my team. I was fallible; I had made some mistakes and, fortunately, I learned from them. The absolute worst scenario would be to go through a humbling experience and to come out of it on the other side as arrogant or more arrogant than before. We are all fallible. In our mistakes and imperfections, we are even stronger, better equipped leaders than ever before. When we accept our shortcomings, we are more able to accept them in others. When we allow our egos to overly guide us, we miss the real opportunities to connect with people and to be more powerful leaders.

Leadership and learning are indispensable to each other.

—John F. Kennedy

Be Consistent and Clear

When we think of parenting, the word discipline always comes up. I had a difficult time with this word because I thought it was synonymous with punishment. Punishment for me meant obedience, and I didn't want to raise an obedient child. I wanted to raise a child who was a thinking child and who could discern for herself. I wanted my child to be able to make her own decisions based on the foundations of right and wrong. Obedience implies a rote "following" of someone else's lead as opposed to being self-directed. When I internalized that discipline really meant establishing boundaries and regulating behavior with consistency and clarity, I was home free.

The leap to leadership on this one is so clear. If we think about leadership in the antiquated command and con-

But as leaders of the 21st century, we are more guiding leaders rather than directing leaders; we want to serve our associates on our journey to greatness. With this understanding of leadership, discipline takes on a more guiding and regulating definition whose purpose it is to develop guardrails and expectations for success.

trol manner, then we do equate discipline with punishment. But as leaders of the 21st century, we are more guiding leaders rather than directing leaders; we want to serve our associates on our journey to greatness. With this understanding of leadership, discipline takes on a more guiding and regulating definition whose purpose it is to develop guardrails and expectations for success. Under this new view of discipline, the need for consistency and clarity is essential.

Unfortunately, we still see leaders today who say one thing and do another. They don't "walk the talk," or the words and the pictures don't match. It's like seeing a movie where the sound track is just a bit off. They lack consistency. You can't establish expectations for success without consistency and clarity for both actions and words.

I learned that with a three year old, you have to say something, do it, and then say it again. This builds trust. Consistency and clarity help build the trust that a leader needs. Every time I need to do something that didn't involve my child, I would say something like this: "Mom is going to go outside to check the mail, and I will be right back." So I went outside, checked the mail and came back in, and said: "Mom went outside to check the mail, and I came right back." This consistent and clear communication helps build trust that allows me to discipline my child regarding wrong and right behaviors. She is much more inclined to listen to me because we have already established trust through a pattern of consistency and clarity. If we were to take this approach into the workplace, it might look something like this.

"Team, you have set forth a great plan to address our decline in market share, and I know that it requires a significant investment. Since the financials are sound, I will review it with the CFO and report back on next steps." I then go and see the CFO. After I do so, I call a meeting to update the team. "Team, I reviewed your plan with the CFO, and I wanted to report back on his perspective which should outline our next steps." I can tell you that many leaders in my career may have followed through on their commitment to go and discuss the plan with the CFO, but they forgot to close the loop with the team by reporting back.

What if I went out to get the mail and came back a hour later? Do you think that my daughter would trust me? When leaders don't follow through, we lose trust. When we lose trust, we can't lead. Are you consistent in your communication? Are you clear on the actions that you will take? Do you follow through?

When I was leading a fairly large team of cross-functional members, we were asked by senior management to introduce a new line of beverages that would meet the needs of the school market. My team resisted and laid out many reasons for why we shouldn't introduce this new line of beverages. I agreed with their assessment and assured the team that I would represent this collective point of view to senior management. They were relieved, and they were excited that I had believed in their analysis and was willing to go to bat for them. I told them that I would review the information and return with a full update. When I went to our leadership meeting to discuss the state of the business and to review the proposal of introducing this new line of beverages, I was presented with a great deal of new information that caused me to see this senior management request in a totally new light. As I sat in the meeting, I saw that the analysis that my team had so diligently prepared was no longer relevant given this new information. The meeting went on for two days. When I came out of the meeting, there was much to tell the team. But in the interest of time and in the urgency I felt coming out of the meeting, I made a grave mistake and made my communication short and to the point.

"Team, we are going to launch this new product line. We need to get on it right away. It is important that we meet the timelines that senior management has given us, so we need to get on with it ASAP." There was stunned silence in the room. One of my associates then raised her hand and quietly asked, "So they didn't agree with our analysis?" I said, "I learned a great deal of new information at the meeting that made our perspective no longer relevant to share with senior management. There are a great deal of business issues going on right now, and we just need to move forward and get going with their request."

What I didn't recognize at that point in time was that I broke trust in a huge way. I didn't do what I told them I was going to do, and I left out a great deal of information that could have allowed them to better understand the context of my "selling out." From their point of view, I had abandoned them and left them to be washed out to sea. I was neither consistent nor clear in my communication. In this situation, I should have taken the time to sit with my team and go through the details of the meeting. I owed them that. They had to come to the same conclusions that I had over the course of those two days in order to understand the decision and to move forward with the swiftness and passion that were needed.

> **Time and stress can also be our enemies in being consistent and clear. It takes real focus and real commitment to want to communicate consistently and clearly. It means that nothing is more important than the people in front of you. The stresses of the day, the timelines pushing on us, none of it is as important.**

Integrity also plays an important role when we are striving for consistency and clarity. Great leaders have integrity. I am defining integrity to be more than just telling the truth. Integrity is about standing up for what you believe in. A great leader has the courage and conviction to go against the grain and do the right thing.

Where I lacked integrity in this example was when I decided not to go forward and present my team's work. While I believed at the time that the information was out of context, I gave up my word far too easily when faced with new data and perspectives. If I really believed their perspective was valid before the meeting, then I should have stood by it.

The truth is that I was only half-heartedly convinced of their recommendation and my commitment to the team was not made with integrity. If I had the conviction and belief in the recommendation, then I probably would have been able to follow through and been more consistent and clear. You can see that when a leader has integrity to stand up for what they believe in, consistency and clarity are facilitated. As leaders, when we commit, we must fully commit with 100 percent conviction. When we don't, we risk breaking trust.

Time and stress can also be our enemies in being consistent and clear. It takes real focus and real commitment to want to communicate consistently and clearly. It means that nothing is more important than the people in front of you. The stresses of the day, the timelines pushing on us, none of it is as important.

I have learned that nothing is so important to break trust with my daughter. She can be late to school if she has a meltdown. I can delay the start of a project if need be. We can alter our plans if necessary, but I won't gloss over consistency and clarity because of these pressures. I don't enjoy being late, and I am not endorsing that we start making excuses. However, we need to take these opportunities when they are right in front of us to value those around us in a consistent and clear way. It takes months and years to build trust and it only takes one action to break it.

What about you? Are you consistent and clear? Do you make commitments with conviction? Are you willing to stand up for your beliefs with integrity? Or, do you allow yourself to make half-hearted commitments? Do the pressures of the day and the stress of time allow you to gloss over the important details that can break trust?

Leadership offers an opportunity to make a difference in someone's life no matter what the project.

—Bill Owens

Be Vulnerable and Give of Yourself

Ｎone of the preceding insights can work without this last insight: be vulnerable and give of yourself. As I said in one of the earlier chapters, it all starts with bringing your heart to work. If you can't bring your heart to work, do yourself a favor and find another company, job or career where you can. You might not be where you should be. You might not be doing what you were called to do. But it is not enough to just bring your heart to work; you have to use it. You have to be vulnerable and share a piece of yourself. Your heart allows you to believe, to be curious, to be receptive, and to practice all seven insights for effective leadership. I believe that you absolutely cannot be a leader who people willingly want to follow without committing a big piece of yourself.

> It is only through our hearts that we connect personally and we fully engage people. If you are leading from your head, you might be directing folks, you might be setting strategy, and you might think you are leading, but you probably don't have a great number of willing followers.

It is only through our hearts that we connect personally and we fully engage people. If you are leading from your head, you might be directing folks, you might be setting strategy, and you might think you are leading, but you probably don't have a great number of willing followers. True leaders are people who others seek out. They really want to be on your team. Leading with our hearts is probably one of the most difficult things to do. The reason it is so difficult is because it is so counter to everything we learn in life. Leading with your heart implies that it is through vulnerability that we find power. Leading from the heart takes an incredible amount of courage.

Vulnerability is all about exposure, and exposure is scary with even our closest friends and family. When we expose ourselves, it fundamentally requires a great deal of strength. We don't want others to use our openness and vulnerability against us. I am not suggesting that you have to tell the stories that still fill you with pain or anger, but tell the stories that have lived within you long enough that you can share your lessons to inspire and motivate others. In a large corporate environment, it is difficult and scary to feel exposed. There is a leap of faith both in yourself and in your organization when you open up. The key to this is to really get in touch with your core beliefs. Our core beliefs really drive who we are as individuals. They define our motives and our hearts.

I said earlier that Don Knauss was the one true leader I had encountered in my career. One of his core beliefs is, "Most people want to do their best work." This core belief drove everything I saw in Don. He connected this belief to his messages about innovation, organizational change, and diversity. This belief is why he took the time to know the person's name who changed his office light bulbs. He believed that people wanted to have pride in what they did so that they could be valued for their best. He touched many people's hearts with this unwavering core belief. When a core belief is so palpable that everyone can see it, you know that a leader is a living example of what is in their heart. You only need to speak to the people in the Minute Maid division at The Coca-Cola Company to understand that many people's sentiments about Don would be the same as mine. This is true leadership via the heart. Vulnerability might be more achievable for folks if they latched onto a core belief and shared it openly and passionately with their people. Don had great passion for leadership, and we all knew it. People knew that he wasn't just doing a job, but that he really cared. He was present with all of us.

When Don had to make a tough decision to let a lot of people go, he took the time to call the entire organization together to deliver a consistent and clear message. He told us about how he personally struggled with the choice, and he shared the options he considered. People could respect the decisions he had to make. He shared his pain, and we knew that he was like a father who sat down with his family to tell them why they had to move out of the big house because of his job loss. Don conducted this meeting with such vulnerability and humanity that people wanted to give him a standing ovation even though he had just delivered an incredibly heart-wrenching message that would change people's lives. He had given so much of himself that his pain for those whose lives were going to change was evident, yet he was strong, confident, clear and consistent in letting us know why this was the course we had to take.

Bravo! What an incredible leader. People use the word "love" when they speak about Don. His team loved him because he loved his team. Vulnerability gave him power, but it was the kind of power that transforms rather than abuses.

I know that I strive to be the kind of leader that Don was for me. Vulnerability is not easy, especially when we think that power is about strength and control. A mindset shift is again required to understand how vulnerability can bring power. When we bring our full selves to the table, our associates see us as real people, just like they are. We relate to people, not robots. We connect with people who are able to connect with us on a deeper level than our heads will allow. Leaders are often cast into a non-human light. Like a celebrity or politician, we suddenly think that they aren't like the rest of us. Leading can be lonely because people might stop speaking to you freely. It is up to the leader to open the doorway. Leaders *must* show vulnerability in order for people to connect with them. Leaders who don't realize they are no longer just the person down the hall can fail to see why people don't come to the corner office to speak with them any more. Or they have the illusion that they have an "open door" policy when in reality nobody would dare pass through it. Leaders need to take the step to open themselves up so that their team members can see them as approachable and real. The steps include being vulnerable and sharing your stories.

As I said at the beginning of the book, I came from a generation of folks who shielded themselves from those they worked with. We kept our distance, and we checked our hearts at the door. Seeing vulnerability as a positive thing was foreign to me. I didn't realize that what I was doing was increasing the distance from folks. I thought that it was important to maintain an image of someone who was in control. I never dreamed it would have the opposite effect, but it did.

> **Seeing vulnerability as a positive thing was foreign to me. I didn't realize that what I was doing was increasing the distance from folks. I thought that it was important to maintain an image of someone who was in control. I never dreamed it would have the opposite effect, but it did.**

One time I considered opening up my home to the women associates in marketing. A fellow woman colleague and I thought establishing regular events with more junior women would be a great way to help mentor others. I thought this might be a good step since I always wanted to reach back and help other women succeed. I decided to host a "women in marketing" event at my house.

I was nervous. I was really nervous. I had never done anything like this before, and I felt I would be exposed on some level. At the time, I was single and I lived alone. My home was such a separate part of myself. It was not that I had anything to hide. It was that I wasn't sure I wanted to open myself up to these folks who weren't close friends. Even though I am an extrovert, my home had ways been my private respite, and this was especially the case when I was single. We ended up having a wonderful time. There were moments, however, when I found myself uncomfortable with many of the questions that kept coming up. One in particular kept surfacing as we sat outside on my back deck. My deck overlooked a lovely backyard with a detached garage. I lived in a historic part of Houston, and my home was built in the early '20s. Detached garages were common in the neighborhood. I had converted my garage into a dance studio, because dance has and always will be a great passion of mine.

The question was, "Laura, what is back in your garage? It looks like someone lives there. Is that an apartment or is it a garage?" Now this would not be a threatening question to most folks. The reason it was for me was because it was going to open up a part of me to these folks that I had never shared with colleagues at work. I found myself stumbling on the question.

"Well, uhhh, it is a garage," I said. "A garage with curtains?" they responded. "Well, not exactly," I said. After a big, long, deep breath I said, "It is a dance studio."

Silence ensued. My work associates struggled to understand why in the world I, their work-around-the-clock, ambitious and driven leader, would have a dance studio in her back yard.

"Dancing is my passion," I said through the silence. There it was, and I had said it. I put it out there, and I quickly realized that they were very intrigued. A sense of elation and excitement came over me. Before I knew it, I was saying, "I will go get the keys. Let's go see it. I want to show you my dance studio." They clamored in unison, "Oh yes! Let's go see it. How exciting!"

As we entered my private space, my heart raced, not with fear but excitement. They were all taken aback with the beauty of my dance studio, and it was obvious to them that my heart lived there. They wanted to know all about it. When did you start dancing? What kind of dance do you do? Do you teach here? Do you perform? For the first time in my career, a piece of the real me had been shared.

Then one of my associates said to me, "Wow, Laura, you need to be on Oprah! You are the kind of woman she features. You know the kind of powerful woman leader who has the balance in her life we are all striving for. You're a dancer and a corporate executive!" I was so incredibly humbled and inspired by that comment, not because I wanted to be on Oprah, but because they saw the real me in a more holilstic light. My fear of exposing myself was invalid. It turned out that by unveiling a piece of myself, they had a deeper sense of appreciation for all of me. I now could be a better role model than ever before.

It was an amazing lesson. That was the beginning of my journey of becoming a connected and committed leader. I knew that once I was able to bring my heart to work, to be vulnerable and to be committed to the other insights, that I would be the type of leader I had hoped to become. With these insights, I felt that I could touch other people's hearts in ways that could transform them to become better leaders themselves. This is my hope and my dream for you.

PART III

TAKING ACTION

Everthing that can be counted does not necessarily count; everything that counts cannot necessarily be counted.

—Albert Einstein

PART III

Lead in All Directions

When we lead, we need to lead in all directions: up, down and sideways. As leaders, we don't always remember this. We can get myopic and forget that people in all directions can help us achieve our goals through great leadership. If we are not careful, we can impede our efforts. Leadership is often thought of as something that works downward to the employees who "work for us," but it is really much more broad-reaching. In fact, in the true definition of leadership, there is no up, down or sideways, because leadership is not imposed by a role. As a leader in all aspects in life, we are the single point of the inverted pyramid, and we serve others. When we lead in this fashion, we are not telling people what to do; they are doing things that support us because we serve them. We all benefit and get what we need. Leadership is a mindset that is not constrained by a traditional hierarchy.

> As a leader in all aspects in life, we are the single point of the inverted pyramid, and we serve others. When we lead in this fashion, we are not telling people what to do; they are doing things that support us because we serve them.

Through my humbling experiences, I learned the concept of leading in all directions. I used to single-mindedly focus on my team and my business. However, I was part of a much bigger whole that I dismissed. My view did not include the broader group. I didn't treat others beside me and above me with the respect and service they deserved. I was fallible for not fully capturing the true essence of leadership.

When we embody the insights of a true leader, we aren't selective about who will receive our leadership qualities. There is no selection. If we are selecting the few that we believe "in" or the few that we chose to be curious about, then we are back to square one and we are not using all of the insights in a consistent and clear manner. We don't see the forest through the trees. We focus our efforts in one direction and the rest is disregarded. How could you be a leader if you are only leading a few and leaving the others behind? You can't. Leadership is not something that we dabble in; it requires full commitment and connection across the board.

> **Turf leadership is arrogant and self-centered. Matrix organizations try to solve this with structure and dual-reporting relationships.**

I believed that if I kept my team informed, shared a bit of myself, was receptive and real with them, then I was a leader. How much of a leader was I if I limited access to a non-team member to my business? Not much of one.

In large corporations, if you are leading your business and your team as if you were alone on a deserted island, your business and team will ultimately suffer. Turf leadership is not leadership. It goes against the foundation of a connected and committed leader. Turf leadership denies the fundamental fact that in business we are dependent on each other. A connected leader understands this. Sales needs Marketing. Marketing needs Finance. Finance needs Manufacturing. And Manufacturing needs Sales. Turf leadership is arrogant and self-centered. Matrix organizations try to solve this with structure and dual-reporting relationships. While dual reporting can have its merits, it does not fully solve the turf issue. At the heart of turf leadership is the belief that no one is valued unless they are on my team, supporting my business. This is a recipe for disaster; the result is a business operating in vacuums.

Unfortunately, we see turf wars in corporations all of the time. Everyone knows it isn't effective, and yet it is prevalent within and across industries. At the root of this behavior is fear and mistrust. We develop turfs as a way to feel secure and a way to enhance our perceived control and power. When organizations have issues with excessive turf wars, there is a fundamental problem with trust. Mistrust can exist in all directions. When we have mistrust horizontally across an organization, it is likely there is mistrust vertically, too.

Trust can be rebuilt by practicing each of the connected and committed leader insights. A connected and committed leader's focus is to ensure trust so that they can lead. Leadership is impossible if trust is absent. After all, leadership skills are human relating skills, so how can you employ them if no relationship exists?

> A connected and committed leader's focus is to ensure trust so that they can lead. Leadership is impossible if trust is absent. After all, leadership skills are human relating skills, so how can you employ them if no relationship exists?

It helps to bring some clarity by comparing a parenting example. Turf wars can happen within families. They often are driven by the two parents.

A personal story is best here. When Leila first came home, it was clear that Lewis and I needed to adjust our relationship to incorporate a third being. We have very different personal styles of parenting. I am more nurturing and able to see more gray. He, on the other hand, is quite black and white. After all, he is an engineer! Thankfully, we have a solid foundation of shared beliefs. However, we often have to remind ourselves because our styles are so diametrically opposed. We can get tangled up when we only see the surface of our actions without understanding that our intentions, hopes and desires come from the same foundation. Our anxiety was heightened, as most new parents experience, so our understanding of our style differences was not at its highest level.

When we are under pressure, it is easy to default to believing that our way is the right way and to lose our compassion for another's perspective. When Leila hit the terrible twos, we were in one of those stressful periods. The turf war ensued a bit like this:

Laura: If I hear her say "no" one more time, I think I am going to go crazy.

Lewis: Well, you know, she doesn't do that with me.

Laura: She doesn't? I don't see that she acts any differently with you.

Lewis: Just let her be. You keep forcing things on her. Of course she is going to say no.

Laura: What are you talking about? I don't force things on her. She responds very well to me.

> *Lewis:* I think she is more agreeable with me.
> I don't force things on her, and I am
> clearer with her.

This was the classic argument on whose way was the best way. Fortunately, we didn't bring our daughter into it, which is what happens in a true turf war. Those who are brought in end up walking on eggshells around the two who have created the turf war. The behaviors of a turf war, whether at home or at work, are very similar. We weren't listening to each other. We didn't believe in each other. We weren't curious about each other's approach. We were defensive and holding onto our ground. The conversation went nowhere. This is what often happens in large corporations with turf wars. Nobody learns from the other, and everybody resorts to doing it their way, and business goes nowhere.

In classic turf wars in corporations, we see many projects that deal with the same issue that is being addressed in various parts of the organization. One time in my career, we were pushing hard at getting a new bottle shape implemented for our brand, Minute Maid Lemonade. The reasons for this initiative, from a marketing point of view, were clear: our target consumer preferred the bottle both aesthetically and functionally. The new bottle provided some real benefits to the consumer. We worked with research and development and manufacturing to ensure that we could develop the best bottle to deliver what the consumer wanted. So far, so good.

In one of our conversations with the manufacturing folks, we learned that there were other brand initiatives that were looking to do the same thing for other brands. One thing about brand folks is that we are all myopic about our brands. Our brand and our core consumer is all that we care about. You could just imagine the conversation that ensued between the various brand groups. It was a bit like the one between my husband and me. The conversation went nowhere. While there was some give and take, in the end, we each continued with our own new bottle initiative. Manufacturing kept screaming that we couldn't support all these different and new bottles, but marketing didn't care.

We each wanted our bottle and our initiative to be the one that would go forward. Some turf wars, like this one, can be mitigated by having the right incentives in place. In the end, brand folks are responsible for growing their brand, not some other brand. In this example, the marketing folks had one boss who ultimately ruled on whose bottle would go forward and whose didn't. Even if they work for the same company and want the whole company to grow, they still are focused on their small piece. Turfs are blinding. By opening up our eyes to see broader goals and broader areas of influence, we can start being more effective leaders.

What my brand team and I didn't realize was that even if we couldn't get our initiative done and a larger brand team did, the company would still win and so would we. However, the team lacked the confidence that the company would be fair with us. We were scared of being reprimanded for not being able to make our initiative happen, even if the broader company won. Organizations with turf wars require a heavy focus on the broader metrics in addition to individual group metrics. But it all needs to be embedded into an organization that has trust flowing in all directions.

When we start to practice the key insights that I have outlined in this book, we can begin to treat each other with respect and to build trust. We do this one person at a time, horizontally and vertically within an organization. We must remember that it is not sufficient to lead our teams, but we must be leaders in all directions. Leadership enables and mobilizes entire organizations, not just one unit or one department.

Leadership is a privilege to better the lives of others.

—**Mwai Kibaki**

PART III

Conclusion

When you bring all seven insights into play, you need to use each of them consistently in all directions. However, it is important to understand your base line on each of these dimensions. Your first priority should be to get a realistic picture on the impact you are having on others across each of the insights. Rate yourself-honestly on the continuum below. Conduct this assessment several times, once for each direction: down, up and across your organization. You might find that you are doing great in one direction, but need help in another direction. Remember a connected and committed leader is consistently applying these insights in all directions.

Insight #1: Believe and Let Go		
I believe in the ability of others and let them do it.	I am a bit skeptical about what others can do for me, so I check in frequently.	No one can do it quite like me. I am involved from start to finish without a lot of input.
5 Points	3 Points	1 Point

Insight #2: Be Curious and See Everyone

I am intrigued by others' perspectives, so I willingly invite them to share.	I am a bit interested in what others have to say. I sometimes invite them to share.	I'd rather deal with those that see it my way. My time is too precious to waste on differing viewpoints.
5 Points	3 Points	1 Point

Insight #3: Be Receptive and Yield

My role as a leader is to guide and motivate others to bring solutions.	My role as a leader is to guide my team to reach consensus and do things how I want them done.	My role as a leader is to have the answers and to tell others what to do.
5 Points	3 Points	1 Point

Insight #4: Be Real and Serve

I have succeeded as a leader only if others have achieved their goals.	I have succeeded as a leader when I reach my goals. Others might reach their goals, but this isn't as critical as meeting mine.	I have succeeded as a leader when I reach my goals regardless of what the impact is on others' goals.
5 Points	3 Points	1 Point

Insight #5: Be Humble and Keep your Ego in Check		
Leadership is a privilege and an important responsibility. I won't ask anything of my team that I won't do myself.	Leadership sometimes requires having others do what I would never do. My time is too valuable.	Leadership has its privileges. I don't have to abide by the same rules or do the same things that I ask of others.
5 Points	3 Points	1 Point

Insight #6: Be Consistent and Clear		
My actions fully support my words.	I try, but I am not always consistently saying and doing the same.	My words and actions don't match.
5 Points	3 Points	1 Point

Insight #7: Be Vulnerable and Give of Yourself		
I share a great deal with my team about who I am beyond the role that I fill.	I share some about who I am with my team but not always with everyone.	My personal life and stories are not important to share with others at work.
5 Points	3 Points	1 Point

Total Points

35-30 points—You are walking on water. You are the ultimate Connected and Committed Leader. Congratulations! However, it is not a bad idea to confirm and validate your rating through the eyes of others. I recommend a 360 feedback with your team using this form.

29-20 points—Honesty with yourself is a great policy! It is also a way to get better. You are on your way to becoming a Connected and Committed Leader. Identify your weaker areas and start trying to behave differently in those areas. Enlist others in your journey to further identify ways that your behavior can help benefit you and your results.

19-10 points—Don't give up. You get a great deal of credit for being truthful about your style and approach. You have some rigid ideas that may require some softening, but if you believe in the outcome, you will make the right adjustments to get you on your way to becoming more effective with others.

9 and lower points—You may not want to change. Your viewpoints are too rigid. I guarantee that you can be less stressful in your life if you work at trying to look at a more effective way to work with others and to embrace leadership as an easier way to get the results you want.

After you have completed the assessment, look to others to help validate it. What matters is how others see you as opposed to how you might see yourself. Another key point to keep in mind is that "leaders walk slowly through the crowd." I heard John C. Maxwell say this in a speech once. Maxwell is a New York Times' Bestselling author of *The 21 Irrefutable Laws of Leadership* and *Thinking for a Change*. I love that quote because it is counterintuitive. We often think of leaders as the busy ones or the impatient ones running to the next meeting. Maxwell says that great leaders get to their end goals perhaps a tad slower than others, but they get there with others. When you are running through the crowd, you might be able to get whereever you are going faster, but you usually get there alone. A connected and committed leader is voluntarily followed. They never reach their goals alone. Following these seven insights require you to "walk slowly through the crowd."

Step out of your comfort zone to lead. I haven't always done this, and I regularly practice at perfecting my own seven leadership insights at home as I do at work. I made a commitment to leadership by writing this book. I hope you will agree that I brought my heart into the work of writing this book, and that my doing so is one step in the process of encouraging you to do the same. I hope that it stirred something in you and motivated you to be the best leader you have the ability to be.

Stories, I have come to understand, are great tools for enabling us to become better leaders. The connected and committed leader's seven leadership insights require us to give a piece of ourselves to better lead others. Our stories help share who we are, and encourage others to do the same. How we have become who we are will help guide others on their not-so-different journeys. Please use these insights coupled with your own personal stories to help teach and lead others.

You can't expect others to do what you are unwilling to do yourself. If you want to lead, you have to take the first step. If you want others to be engaged and to bring their hearts, you have to go first.

With this book, I decided to go first. I hope you go first with someone else. Join me in being a catalyst for better leadership in our lives. We can bring back the humanity, the creativity, the inclusiveness and the spark in our lives, both at work and at home. And remember, it all begins and ends with leadership.

Bibliography

Bossidy, Larry, Ram Charan, and Charles Burck. *Execution: The Discipline of Getting Things Done*. New York: Crown Business, 2002.

Collins, Jim. *Good to Great,* New York: Harper Business, 2001.

Covey, Stephen. *The 7 Habits of Highly Effective People.* New York: Simon & Schuster, 1989.

Dotlich, David L. and Peter C. Cairo. *Why CEOs Fail: The 11 Behaviors That Can Derail Your Climb to the Top And How to Manage Them.* San Francisco: Jossey-Bass, 2003

Glaser, Judith. *The DNA of Leadership. Leverage your instincts to: Communicate, Differentiate and Innovate.* Avon, MA: Platinum Press, 2006.

Hunter, James C. *The Servant: A Simple Story About the True Essence of Leadership.* Rocklin, CA: Prima Publishing, 1998.

Maxwell, John C. *The Irrefutable Laws of Leadership.* Georgia: Maxwell Motivation, Inc., 2002.

Maxwell, John C. *Thinking for a Change: 11 Ways Highly Successful People Approach Life and Work.* New York: Warner Business Books, 2003.

Smith, Anthony F. *The Taboos of Leadership: The 10 Secrets No One Will Tell You About Leaders and What They Really Think.* San Francisco, CA: Jossey-Bass, 2007.

Winget, Larry. *It's Called Work For a Reason! Your Success is Your Own Damn Fault.* New York: Gotham Books, 2007.

www.LivingLeadershipPress.com